2008-2009 Workbook for

Evolve Review
Live Review Course for the
NCLEX-RN® Exam

ELSEVIER

ELSEVIER

11830 Westline Industrial Drive
St. Louis, Missouri 63146

2008-2009 Workbook for Evolve Review
Live Review Course for the NCLEX-RN® Exam

ISBN: 978-1-4377-0171-5

NOTICE

NCLEX®, NCLEX-RN®, and NCLEX-PN® are registered trademarks of the National Council of State Boards of Nursing, Inc.

International Standard Book Number: 978-1-4377-0171-5

Managing Editor: Nancy L. O'Brien
Publishing Services Manager: Deborah L. Vogel
Senior Project Manager: Ann E. Rogers
Design Direction: Amy Buxton

Printed in United States of America

Last digit is the print number: 9   8   7   6   5   4   3   2   1

Contributing Authors

Susan Morrison, PhD, RN
President Emerita
Elsevier Review and Testing
Nursing and Health Professions
Houston, Texas

Ainslie Nibert, PhD, RN
Vice President
Elsevier Review and Testing
Nursing and Health Professions
Houston, Texas

Mickie Hinds, PhD, RN
Director, Review and Curriculum
Elsevier Review and Testing
Nursing and Health Professions
Houston, Texas

Judy R. Hyland, MS, RN
Manager, Review and Curriculum
Elsevier Review and Testing
Nursing and Health Professions
Houston, Texas

Judy Siefert, MSN, RN
Director, Testing
Elsevier Review and Testing
Nursing and Health Professions
Houston, Texas

Denise Voyles, BSN, RN
Testing Manager
Elsevier Review and Testing
Nursing and Health Professions
Houston, Texas

Illustration Credits

Chapter 5: Medical-Surgical Nursing
(Page 60)
Lewis SM, Heitkemper MM, O'Brien PG, Bucher L: *Medical-Surgical Nursing: Assessment and Management of Clinical Problems*, ed 7, St Louis, 2007, Mosby.

(Page 82)
Hockenberry MJ, Wilson D: *Nursing Care of Infants and Children*, ed 8, St Louis, 2007, Mosby.

Chapter 6: Pediatric Nursing
(Pages 89-93)
Hockenberry MJ, Wilson D: *Nursing Care of Infants and Children*, ed 8, St Louis, 2007, Mosby.

Chapter 7: Maternal/Newborn Nursing
(Page 122)
Lowdermilk DL, Perry SE: *Maternity and Women's Health Care*, ed 9, St Louis, 2007, Mosby.

Contents

 **Introduction**

Welcome to the Elsevier Evolve Live Review Course

This series of slides and workbook provide test-taking strategies and a content review of nursing curriculum to help prepare nursing students for the NCLEX-RN Examination. If students want a more in-depth review of certain material please refer to:

- *Evolve Reach Comprehensive Review for the NCLEX-RN Examination* (powered by HESI)
- *Mosby's Comprehensive Review of Nursing for NCLEX-RN Examination*
- *Saunders Comprehensive Review for the NCLEX-RN Examination*

Knowledge is Power!

- Enhance test-taking skills
- Review basic curriculum content
- Organize knowledge
- Identify content weakness
- Know what to expect

NCLEX-RN EXAMINATION

- Safe and Effective Practice
- "Essential" Nursing Knowledge
- **Think: safety, *safety*, SAFETY!**

Nursing Process

- Planning and implementing nursing care based on assessment, diagnosis, and determining priorities
- Evaluating the effectiveness of nursing care

Client Needs

- Safe and effective care environment
    — Management of care
    — Safety and infection control
- Health promotion and maintenance
- Psychosocial integrity
- Physiological integrity
    — Basic care and comfort
    — Pharmacological and parenteral therapies
    — Reduction of risk potential
    — Physiological adaptation

NCLEX-RN TEST PLAN

- The Test Plan is revised every 3 years after conducting a practice analysis with entry-level nurses.
- Information about the Test Plan including descriptions of content categories and related content for each category can be found at www.ncsbn.org.
- This site also contains information for students, frequently asked questions, and examples of alternate formats.

TEST-TAKING STRATEGIES

- ABCs
- Maslow's Hierarchy of Needs
- Start with least invasive intervention
- Assess before taking action, when appropriate
- Have all the necessary information/take all possible relevant actions before calling the physician/healthcare provider
- Which client to assess first (most at risk, most physiologically unstable)

Strategies for Success: Four Essential Steps

1. Determine if the style of the question is

$$+ \text{ positive } +$$
$$\text{or}$$
$$- \text{ negative } -$$

2. Find the key words in the question
3. Rephrase the question in your own words
4. Rule out options

Determine if the question is written in a positive or negative style

- A *positive* style may ask what the nurse should *do,* or the best or first action to implement.
- A *negative* style may ask what the nurse should avoid, which prescription the nurse should question, or which behavior indicates the need for re-teaching the client.

Find the key words in the question

- Ask yourself which words or phrases provide the critical information?
- This information may be the age of the client, the setting, the timing, a set of symptoms or behaviors, or any number of other factors.
- For example, the nursing actions for a 10-year-old 1-day postop client are different from those for a 70-year-old 1-hour postop client.

Rephrase the question in your own words

- This will help you eliminate nonessential information in the question and help you determine the correct answer.
- Ask yourself, "What is this instructor *really* asking?"
- Before looking at the choices, rephrase the question in your own words and answer the question.

Rule out options

- Based on your knowledge, you can probably identify one or two options that are clearly incorrect.
- Mentally mark through those options on the computer monitor.
- Now, differentiate between the remaining options, considering your knowledge of the subject and related nursing principles, such as roles of the nurse, nursing process, ABCs, and Maslow's Hierarchy of Needs.

A client who has COPD is resting in semi-Fowler's position with oxygen at 2 liters/minute per nasal cannula. The client develops dyspnea. What action should the nurse implement first?
A. Call the healthcare provider
B. Obtain a bedside pulse oximeter
C. Raise the head of the bed further
D. Assess the client's vital signs

Rationales:

A. *Call the healthcare provider*
Immediate action and further assessment should be completed before notifying the healthcare provider.

B. *Obtain a bedside pulse oximeter*
This should provide valuable assessment data, but will not reduce the client's dyspnea.

C. *Raise the head of the bed further*
This action should be implemented first and is most likely to provide immediate benefit for the client.

D. *Assess the client's vital signs*
Assessment is not always first if enough information is available to take immediate action to benefit the client.

The stem of the question may contain *"Red Flag Words."*
Practice rewording the questions below:

1. "Which response indicates to the nurse a need to *re-teach* the client about ..."
(Which information/understanding by the client is incorrect?)

2. "Which prescription (order) should the nurse *question*?"
(Which prescription is unsafe, not beneficial, inappropriate to this client situation, etc.?)

Test-Taking Strategies: Opposites in the answer:
- Examples of opposites are prone/supine, elevated/decreased.
- Read VERY carefully; one is likely to be the answer, BUT not always.
- If you do not know the answer, choose the most likely of the "opposites" and move on.

1. Is the item written in a positive or a negative style?

2. Find the key words in the question.

3. Rephrase the question in your own words.

4. Rule out options:
-
-
-

Unless there is fluid overload ...
Common interventions include:
- Small, frequent feedings
- Recommended fluid intake: "3 liters/day"
- Alternate rest with activity
- Conserve energy with any activity

Look for TEACHING POINTS and "teachable moments"
- Risk factors: known modifiable vs. nonmodifiable
- Prevention and wellness promotion
- New meds/self-care instructions
- Client empowerment
- *Anticipatory* guidance
- Incorporating within client's **lifestyle, culture, spiritual beliefs,** etc.

More Test-Taking Strategies: A Few Words About "Words"
- Healthcare provider: the person prescribing care (e.g., physician, nurse practitioner)
  — Physician = "doctor"
  — Prescriptions = "orders"
- Unlicensed assistive personnel
  — Patient care technician
  — Nursing assistant
  — Nurse's aide

Use reasoning; keep memorizing to a minimum
- Growth and developmental milestones
- Death and dying stages
- Crisis intervention
- Immunizations/*drug classifications*
- Principles of teaching/learning
- Stages of pregnancy and fetal growth
- *Nurse Practice Act: Standards of Practice & Delegation*

Know normal ranges for commonly used lab tests (Appendix A), what variations mean, and the BEST nursing actions
- H & H
- WBC, RBC, platelets
- Electrolytes: K^+, Na^+, Ca^{2+}, Mg^{2+}, Cl^-, $PO_4^=$
- BUN and creatinine
- *Relationship* of Ca^{2+} and $PO_4^=$
- ABGs
- PT, INR, PTT (don't get them confused)

A client who has hyperparathyroidism is scheduled to receive a prescribed dose of oral phosphate. The nurse notes that the client's serum calcium level is 12.5 mg/dL. What action should the nurse implement?
A. Hold the phosphate and notify the healthcare provider
B. Review the client's serum parathyroid hormone level
C. Give a PRN dose of IV calcium per protocol
D. Administer the dose of oral phosphate

1. Is the item written in a positive or a negative style?

2. Find the key words in the question.

3. Rephrase the question in your own words.

4. Rule out options:
   -
   -
   -

NUTRITION

Be able to [at least] identify foods relative to their sodium content (high or low), potassium levels (high or low), and increased levels of phosphate, iron, or vitamin K
  — Chemotherapy, GI/GU disturbances
  — Proteins, CHOs, fats
  — Pregnancy and fetal growth needs
- Remember concepts:
  — Introducing one food at a time (infants, allergies)
  — Progression "AS TOLERATED"
- What nursing assessment guides decisions regarding progression?

EVERYTHING YOU NEED TO KNOW ABOUT MEDS

More critical thinking questions are being designed around SKILLS!

Think: safety, *safety*, SAFETY!

Reflect on … the WHOLE PICTURE

Safe medication administration is more than just knowing the action of the med:

- "6 Rights"—five PLUS technique of skill execution
- Drug interactions
- Vulnerable organs: ✓labs; what to assess
- Allergies and presence of suprainfections
- Concept of peak and trough
- How you would know:
  — It's working
  — There's a problem
- Teaching: *safety, empowerment, compliance*

Reflect on: special considerations

- Teratogens
- Vesicants
- Implications of edema, impaired tissue perfusion of injection site
- Hepatorenal status to drug dose/frequency
- Concepts of weaning

Cautionary Tales

DON'T respond based on …

- YOUR past client care experiences or agency
- A familiar phrase or term
- "Of course, *I* would have already …"
- What YOU think is REALISTIC
- YOUR children, pregnancies, parents, elders, personal response to a drug, etc.

DO respond based on …

- ABCs
- Scientific, behavioral, sociologic principles
- Principles of teaching/learning
- Maslow's Hierarchy
- Nursing process
- What's in the stem: no more, no less
- NCLEX-RN ideal hospital
- Basic A&P
- Critical thinking

TEST-TAKING STRATEGIES: TAKE CARE OF YOURSELF

From now until the test:
- DO set up a study schedule and stick to it
- DO avoid negative people
- DO respect your body and your mind
- DO think positively—say to yourself, "I CAN BE SUCCESSFUL!"

The night before the test:
- DO allow only 30 minutes to review test-taking strategies
- DO assemble all necessary materials
  — Admission ticket
  — Directions to testing center
  — Identification
  — Money for lunch
- DO something you enjoy
- DO respect your body and your mind

The day of the test:
- DO allow plenty of time to get there
- DO dress comfortably
- DO take *only* your identification forms into the testing room
- DO avoid distractions
  — Use earplugs if needed
  — Avoid discussing test while waiting to take the exam or during breaks

2 Legal Aspects of Nursing

Topics
- Nurse Practice Acts
- Agency policies
- Incident/adverse occurrence reports
- Torts
  — Unintentional
  — Intentional
- Crimes

The unlicensed assistive personnel (UAP) reports to a staff nurse that a client, who had surgery 4 hours ago, has a decrease in blood pressure (BP) from 150/80 to 110/70 in the last hour. The nurse advises the UAP to check the client's dressing for excess drainage and report the findings to the nurse. Which factor is most important to consider when assessing the legal ramifications of this situation?
A. The parameters of the state's nurse practice act
B. The need to complete an adverse occurrence report
C. Hospital protocols regarding the frequency of vital sign assessment qh postoperatively
D. The physician's prescription regarding changing the postoperative dressing

Psychiatric Nursing
- Admissions
  — Involuntary
  — Emergency
- Client rights
- Competency

1. Is the item written in a positive or a negative style?

2. Find the key words in the question.

3. Rephrase the question in your own words.

4. Rule out options:
   -
   -
   -

What nursing action has the highest priority when admitting a client to a psychiatric unit on an involuntary basis?
A. Reassure the client that this admission is only for a limited amount of time.
B. Offer the client and family the opportunity to share their feelings about the admission.
C. Determine the behaviors that resulted in the need for admission.
D. Advise the client about the legal rights of all hospitalized clients.

1. Is the item written in a positive or a negative style?

2. Find the key words in the question.

3. Rephrase the question in your own words.

4. Rule out options:
   -
   -
   -

Client Identification

- Use at least two client identifiers when taking blood samples, administering medication, or administering blood products.
- The client room number MAY NOT be used for identification.

Consent for Care/Surgery

- Surgical permits
- Consent for treatment
- Minors
- Emergency care
- Healthcare provider's/physician's prescriptions

The nurse enters the room of a preoperative client to obtain the client's signature on the surgical consent form. Which question is most important for the nurse to ask the client?

A. When did the surgeon explain the procedure to you?
B. Is any member of your family going to be here during your surgery?
C. Have you been instructed in postoperative activities and restrictions?
D. Have you received any preoperative pain medication?

1. Is the item written in a positive or a negative style?

2. Find the key words in the question.

3. Rephrase the question in your own words.

4. Rule out options:
   -
   -
   -

Restraints

A family member of a female client who is in a Posey vest restraint asks why the restraint was applied. How should the nurse respond?

A. This restraint was prescribed by the healthcare provider.
B. There is not enough staff to keep her safe all the time.
C. The other patients are upset when she wanders at night.
D. Her actions place her at high risk for harming herself.

1. Is the item written in a positive or a negative style?

2. Find the key words in the question.

3. Rephrase the question in your own words.

4. Rule out options:
   -
   -
   -

Health Insurance Portability and Accountability Act of 1996 (HIPAA)

- HIPAA sets standards regarding the verbal written and electronic exchange of private and sensitive health information.
- HIPAA creates client rights to consent to use and disclose protected health information, to inspect and copy one's medical record, and to amend mistaken or incomplete information.

The standards require all hospitals and health agencies to have specific policies and procedures in place to ensure compliance with the standards.

3 Management/Leadership, Disaster Management, and Bioterrorism

MANAGEMENT/LEADERSHIP

Communication Skills

- "Do it MY way."
  Aggressive communication/authoritarian leader
- "Whatever … as long as you like me."
  Passive communication/laissez-faire leader
- "Let's consider the options available."
  Assertive communication/democratic leader

The charge nurse confronts a staff nurse whose behavior is resentful and negative after a change in unit policy is announced. The staff nurse states, "Don't blame me, nobody likes this idea." What is the charge nurse's priority action?
A. Confront the other staff members involved in the change of unit policy.
B. Call a unit meeting to review the reasons why the change was made.
C. Develop a written unit policy for the expression of complaints.
D. Encourage the nurse to be accountable for her own behavior.

1. Is the item written in a positive or a negative style?

2. Find the key words in the question.

3. Rephrase the question in your own words.

4. Rule out options:
   - ■
   - ■
   - ■

Delegation Skills

Five rights of delegation
- Right task
- Right circumstance
- Right person
- Right direction/communication
- Right supervision

HESI Hints

The functions of assessment, evaluation, and nursing judgment CANNOT be delegated. Remember, RNs delegate to other RNs, PNs, and UAPS specific client care tasks. They retain accountability of the client care. It is the client care manager who assigns clients to nurses. Assignment denotes responsibility to those clients and all of their care needs for the RN. The PN can be assigned specific clients, but the RN retains responsibility for assessment, planning, and teaching responsibilities.

The charge nurse is making assignments for each of four staff members, including a registered nurse (RN), a licensed practical nurse (LPN), and two unlicensed assistive personnel (UAPs). Which task is best to assign the LPN?
A. Maintain a 24-hour urine collection
B. Wean a client from a mechanical ventilator
C. Perform sterile wound irrigation
D. Obtain scheduled vital signs

1. Is the item written in a positive or a negative style?

2. Find the key words in the question.

3. Rephrase the question in your own words.

4. Rule out options:
   - ■
   - ■
   - ■

Supervision Skills

- Direction/guidance
- Evaluation/monitoring
- Follow-up

Which situation warrants a variance (incident) report by the nurse?
A. Refusal by a client to take prescribed medication
B. Improved status before completion of the course of medication
C. An allergic reaction to a prescribed medication
D. A client received medication prescribed for another client

1. **Is the item written in a positive or a negative style?**

2. **Find the key words in the question.**

3. **Rephrase the question in your own words.**

4. **Rule out options:**
   -
   -
   -

DISASTER MANAGEMENT

- The nurse is an active member of teams in the event of biological, chemical, radioactive, mass trauma, and natural disasters.
- The nurse has a role at all three levels of disaster management.

Preparedness ... Response ... Recovery
- Levels of prevention in disaster management
  — *Primary:* planning, training, educating personnel and the public
  — *Secondary:* triage, treatment, shelter supervision
  — *Tertiary:* follow-up, recovery assistance, prevention of future disasters

Triage
- Goal: to maximize number of survivors by sorting the injured as treatable and untreatable, using the criteria of potential for survival and availability of resources
- Color-coded system
- START (Simple Triage And Rapid Treatment) method
  - Separate out walking wounded, move, evaluate later
  - Three-step evaluation of others done one at a time
    — Respiration
    — Circulation
    — Mental status

BIOTERRORISM

- Review exposure information, assessment findings, and treatment for various agents:
  — Biological
  — Chemical
  — Radiation
- Questions may deal with disasters and bioterrorism as they affect the individual victim, families, and the community.

The nurse is completing discharge teaching for a group of postal employees who have been exposed to a powder form of anthrax. Which instruction has the highest priority?
A. Begin the prescribed antibiotics and continue for 60 days.
B. Watch for symptoms of anthrax for the next 7 days.
C. Make arrangements to be vaccinated for anthrax.
D. Explain to family members that anthrax is not contagious.

1. Is the item written in a positive or a negative style?

2. Find the key words in the question.

3. Rephrase the question in your own words.

4. Rule out options:
   ▪
   ▪
   ▪

4 Clinical Concepts, Mechanisms of Disease, Nursing Management, and Clinical Nursing Management

CLINICAL CONCEPTS

Pain

- Pain is whatever the client says it is.
- Pain occurs in all clinical settings.
- Nurses have a central role in pain assessment and management.
  - Assessing pain and communicating to other health care providers
  - Ensuring the initiation and coordination of adequate pain relief measures
  - Evaluating the effectiveness of interventions
  - Advocating for people with pain
- Pain medications generally are divided into three categories.
  - Nonopioids for mild pain
  - Opioids for moderate to severe pain
  - Co-analgesic or adjuvant drugs for neuropathic pain

Types of Pain Medications
Nonopioid Analgesics

- Acetaminophen (Tylenol)
- Salicylates
  - Aspirin
  - Choline magnesium trisalicylate (Trilisate)
- Nonsteroidal anti-inflammatory drugs (NSAIDs)
  - Ibuprofen (Motrin, Nuprin, Advil)
  - Indomethacin (Indocin)
  - Ketorolac (Toradol)
  - Diclofenac K (Cataflam)
- Cyclooxygenase-2 (COX-2) inhibitors
  - Celecoxib (Celebrex)
  - Valdecoxib (Bextra)

Opioid Analgesics

- Mu agonists
  - Morphine (Roxanol, MS Contin, Avinza, Kadian, Epimorph, MSIR, Oramorph SR)
  - Hydromorphone (Dilaudid)
  - Methadone (Dolophine)
  - Levorphanol (Levo-Dromoran)
  - Fentanyl (Sublimaze, Duragesic, Actiq)
  - Oxycodone (Percocet, Percodan, Endocet, Tylox, Roxicodone, OxyContin, Combunox)
  - Hydrocodone (Lortab, Vicodin, Zydone)
  - Codeine (Tylenol No. 3)

HESI Hint

Remember! Naloxone 0.1 mg to 0.4 mg IV can be used to relieve narcotic-induced respiratory suppression.

- Mixed agonist-antagonists
  — Pentazocine (Talwin)
  — Butorphanol (Stadol)
- Partial agonists
  — Buprenorphine (Buprenex)
  — Buprenorphine plus naloxone (Suboxone)

Nonpharmacological Pain Relief Techniques

- Noninvasive
  — Heat and cold application
  — Massage therapy
  — Relaxation techniques
  — Guided imagery
  — Biofeedback techniques
- Invasive
  — Nerve blocks
  — Interruption of neural pathways
  — Acupuncture

Death and Grief

- Stages of grief
  — Denial
  — Anger
  — Bargaining
  — Depression
  — Acceptance
- Encourage client to express anger
- DO NOT take away the defense mechanism/coping mechanism used in crisis
- How families deal with death/dying will vary by culture

MECHANISMS OF DISEASE

Infection

- Infection
  — Invasion of the body by a pathogen
- Response to the invasion
  — Localized
  — Systemic
- Nosocomial infections
  — Acquired as a result of exposure to a microorganism in a hospital setting

Human Immunodeficiency Virus

Routes of Transmission

- Unprotected sexual contact
  — Most common mode of transmission
- Exposure to blood through drug-using equipment
- Perinatal transmission
  — Most common route of infection for children
  — Can occur during pregnancy, at the time of delivery, or after birth through breastfeeding

Symptoms
- May begin with flu-like symptoms in the earliest stage and advance to …
  - Severe weight loss
  - Secondary infections
  - Cancers
  - Neurological disease

HIV Collaborative Management
- Monitoring HIV disease progression and immune function
- Initiating and monitoring antiretroviral therapy (ART)
- Preventing the development of opportunistic diseases
- Detecting and treating opportunistic diseases
- Managing symptoms
- Preventing or decreasing the complications of treatment
- Preventing further transmission of HIV

Ongoing assessment, interactions with the client, and client education and support are required to accomplish these objectives.

HIV Drug Therapy
The goals of drug therapy
- Decrease the viral load
- Maintain or raise CD4+ T-cell counts
- Delay the development of HIV-related symptoms and opportunistic diseases

HIV Medications
- Nucleoside reverse transcriptase inhibitors (NRTIs)
  - Zidovudine (AZT, ZDV, Retrovir)
  - Lamivudine (3TC, Epivir)
  - Abacavir (Ziagen)
  - Emtricitabine (FTC, Emtriva)
- Nucleotide reverse transcriptase inhibitor (NtRTI)
  - Tenofovir DF (Viread)
- Nonnucleoside reverse transcriptase inhibitors (NNRTIs)
  - Enzymes, hepatotoxicity
  - Nevirapine (Viramune)
  - Delavirdine (Rescriptor)
  - Efavirenz (Sustiva)
- Protease inhibitors (PIs)
  - Indinavir (Crixivan)
  - Ritonavir (Norvir)
  - Nelfinavir (Viracept)
  - Amprenavir (Agenerase)
  - Atazanavir (Reyataz)
  - Fosamprenavir (Lexiva)
  - Tipranavir (Aptivus)
  - Darunavir (Prezista)
- Entry inhibitor
  - Enfuvirtide (Fuzeon)

HESI Hint
Pregnant caregivers may choose not to care for a client with cytomegalovirus (CMV).

Pediatric HIV

Common clinical manifestations of HIV infection in children

- Lymphadenopathy
- Hepatosplenomegaly
- Oral candidiasis
- Chronic or recurrent diarrhea
- Failure to thrive
- Developmental delay
- Parotitis

Pediatric Nursing Considerations and Diagnostic Evaluation for HIV

Considerations

- Education concerns transmission and control of infectious diseases.
- Safety issues include appropriate storage of special medications and equipment.
- Prevention is a key component of HIV education.
- Aggressive pain management is essential.
- Common psychosocial concerns include disclosure of the diagnosis.

Evaluation

- For children 18 months of age and older
  - HIV enzyme-linked immunosorbent assay (ELISA)
  - Western blot immunoassay
- For infants younger than 18 months
  - HIV polymerase chain reaction (PCR)

In infants born to HIV-infected mothers, these assays will be positive because of the presence of maternal antibodies derived transplacentally.

Fluid Volume

Fluid Volume Excess

- Causes
  - CHF (most common), renal failure, cirrhosis, overhydration
- Symptoms
  - Peripheral edema, periorbital edema, elevated BP, dyspnea, altered LOC
- Lab findings
  - $\downarrow$ BUN, $\downarrow$ Hgb, $\downarrow$ Hct, $\downarrow$ serum osmolality, $\downarrow$ urine specific gravity
- Treatment
  - Diuretics, fluid restrictions, weigh daily, monitor K^+

Fluid Volume Deficit

- Causes
  - Inadequate fluid intake, hemorrhage, vomiting, diarrhea, massive edema
- Symptoms
  - Weight loss, oliguria, postural hypotension
- Lab findings
  - $\uparrow$ BUN and creatinine, $\uparrow$ Hgb, $\uparrow$ Hct, $\uparrow$ urine specific gravity
- Treatment
  - Strict I & O, replace with isotonic fluids, monitor BP, weigh daily

Electrolyte Balance
- Intracellular
  — K^+ maintains osmotic pressure.
  — K^+ imbalances are potentially life-threatening.
- Extracellular
  — Na^+ maintains most abundant osmotic pressure.
- When there is either ECF or ICF change in concentration, remember that fluid shifts from the area of LESSER concentration to the area of GREATER concentration.

Hyponatremia
- Na^+ <135 mEq/L
- Muscle cramps, confusion
- Check BP frequently
- Restrict fluids, cautious IV replacement as needed

Hypernatremia
- Na^+ >145 mEq/L
- Pulmonary edema, seizures, thirst, fever
- No IVs that contain sodium
- Restrict sodium in diet
- Weigh daily

Hypokalemia
- K^+ <3.5 mEq/L
- Rapid, thready pulse, flat T waves, fatigue, anorexia, muscle cramps
- IV potassium supplements
- Encourage foods high in K^+ (bananas, oranges, spinach)

Hyperkalemia
- K^+ >5.0 mEq/L
- Tall tented T waves, bradycardia, muscle weakness
- 10%-20% glucose with regular insulin
- Kayexalate
- Renal dialysis may be required

Hypocalcemia
- Ca^{++} <8.5 mEq/L
- + Trousseau's sign, + Chvostek's sign, diarrhea, numbness, convulsions
- Administer calcium supplements
- IV calcium give slowly
- Increase dietary calcium

Hypercalcemia
- Ca^{++} >10.5 mEq/L
- Muscle weakness, constipation, nausea and vomiting (N/V), dysrhythmias, behavioral changes
- Limit vitamin D intake
- Avoid calcium-based antacids
- Calcitonin to reduce calcium
- Renal dialysis may be required

Refer to a Review Manual for information regarding hypomagnesemia and hypermagnesemia and hypophosphatemia and hyperphosphatemia:
- *Evolve Reach Comprehensive Review for the NCLEX-RN Examination* (powered by HESI)
- *Mosby's Comprehensive Review of Nursing for NCLEX-RN Examination*
- *Saunders Comprehensive Review for the NCLEX-RN Examination*

IV Therapy

Types of IV fluids

- Isotonic
  0.9% NS, LR, D_5W
- Hypotonic
  0.5% NS, 0.45% NS, $D_{2.5}$ 0.45% NS
- Hypertonic
  D_5 0.45% NS, D_5LR, D_5NS

Hazards of IV Therapy

— Infection
— Pulmonary emboli
— Air emboli
— Circulatory overload
— Phlebitis

Arterial Blood Gas Monitoring

Basics for NCLEX-RN—Interpret ABG results
- pH
  — Normal 7.35 to 7.45
  — <7.35 = acidosis
  — >7.45 = alkalosis
- Pco_2
  — Normal 35 to 45 mm Hg
  — >45 = acidosis
  — <35 = alkalosis
- HCO_3^-
  — Normal 22 to 26 mEq/L
  — <22 = acidosis
  — >26 = alkalosis

NURSING MANAGEMENT

Perioperative Care

Preoperative Care
- Preoperative evaluation
  — Obtain a complete history including
    • List of current meds, and allergies
    • Previous surgical experiences (response to anesthesia)
  — Signed consent
    • Ascertain that informed consent has been obtained prior to patient being sedated
- Preoperative teaching
  — NPO after midnight before surgery
  — Teach coughing and deep breathing, incentive spirometry
  — Review methods of pain control

Intraoperative Care
- Maintain client safety
- Provide psychosocial support
- Immediate postop care
  — Monitoring for S/S of shock
  — Position on side
  — Manage pain

HESI Hint

Know how to calculate the flow rate of an IV.

HESI Hint

Lungs are fast compensators; release excess CO_2 by hyperventilating, retain CO_2 by hypoventilating.
Kidneys regulate bicarbonate and are slow compensators.

NCLEX Reminder

- Review how to determine acid-base disorders
- Think about underlying etiology of each imbalance
  — Respiratory acidosis
  — Metabolic acidosis
  — Respiratory alkalosis
  — Metabolic alkalosis

HESI Hint

NCLEX-RN questions may relate to
- Teaching
- Immediate postoperative care
- Recognizing S/S of complications

Postoperative Care
- Prevent common complications
  - Urinary retention
    - Check for bladder distention
  - Pulmonary problems
    - Check breath sounds
    - O_2 saturation
  - Decreased peristalsis
    - Paralytic ileus
    - Absent bowel sounds
  - Wound dehiscence
  - Wound evisceration

ACUTE CARE NURSING MANAGEMENT

Shock

Stages
- **Stage 1**
  - Early signs include AGITATION
  - Restlessness
  - Increased heart rate
  - Cool pale skin
- **Stage 2**
  - Cardiac output <4–6 L/min
  - BP systolic <100 mm Hg
  - Decreased urinary output
  - Confusion
  - Cerebral perfusion <70
- **Stage 3**
  - Edema
  - Excessively low BP
  - Dysrhythmia
  - Weak thready pulses
- **Stage 4**
  - Profound hypotension
  - Unresponsive to vasopressors
  - Heart rate slows
  - Multiple organ failure
  - Severe hypoxemia

Types
- **Hypovolemic**
  - Most common
  - Related to internal or external blood/fluid loss
- **Cardiogenic**
  - Pump failure
  - Results in ↓ cardiac output
- **Vasogenic**
  - Failure of arteriolar resistance
  - Massive vasodilation and pooling of blood
- **Septic**
  - Endotoxins released from bacteria
  - Massive vasodilation and pooling

HESI Hint
- Cardiogenic shock and pulmonary edema
  - Position patient to REDUCE venous return
  - High Fowler's position with legs down
  - ↓ workload on the heart
  - Help to optimize the O_2 exchange

Treatment for Shock
- **Replace blood volume or fluid loss**
  - — Lactated Ringer's, albumin, whole blood, PRBCs
- Administer medications
  - — Vasodilators
    - Nitroprusside (Nipride)
    - Hydralazine (Apresoline)
    - Labetalol hydrochloride (Normodyne, Trandate)
  - — Vasoconstrictors
    - Dopamine (Dopram)
    - Dobutamine (Dobutrex)
    - Norepinephrine bitartrate (Levophed)
- Monitor
  - — Vital signs
  - — Mental status
  - — Fluid status
  - — Urine output

Hemodynamic Monitoring
- Cardiac output
  - — Cardiac output reflects the blood flow reaching the tissues.
  - — Normal CO is 4–6 L/min.
- Mean arterial pressure (MAP)
  - — Normal MAP is 70 to 100 mm Hg.
  - — MAP is an important indicator of the adequacy of cardiac output.
  - — MAP greater than 60 mm Hg is adequate to maintain perfusion to the vital organs.
- Central venous pressure (CVP)
  - — Normal range is 4–10 cm H_2O.
  - — CVP is a measurement of right ventricular preload.
  - — An elevated CVP indicates right ventricular failure or volume overload.
  - — A low CVP indicates hypovolemia.

Which client should the nurse respond to first?
A. The UAP reports a client with cirrhosis is trying to climb out of bed.
B. A unit clerk relays a message that a wife says her husband is "acting funny."
C. The bedside drainage bag for a client with urinary MRSA who is on strict I & O is leaking.
D. A healthcare provider is insisting the nurse change a soiled stump dressing.

Blood Transfusions
Blood Groups and Types
- The ABO system includes A, B, O, and AB blood types.
- Rh factor is an antigenic substance in the erythrocytes.
- If blood is mismatched during transfusion, a transfusion reaction occurs.
  - — The transfusion reaction is an antigen-antibody reaction.
  - — It can range from a mild response to severe anaphylactic shock.

HESI Hint
 S: Solutions
H: Hemodynamic stability
O: Oxygen
C: Conserve heat
K: Keep feet up and head down

HESI Hint
- All vasopressor and vasodilator drugs are potent and dangerous and require weaning on and off.
- DO NOT change infusion rates simultaneously.
- If BP drop occurs, decrease vasodilator rate first, then increase vasopressor rate.
- If BP increases precipitously, decrease vasopressor rate first, then increase vasodilator rate.

1. **Is the item written in a positive or a negative style?**

2. **Find the key words in the question.**

3. **Rephrase the question in your own words.**

4. **Rule out options:**
   -
   -
   -

Types of Reactions

- Acute hemolytic
- Febrile, nonhemolytic (most common)
- Mild allergic
- Anaphylactic
- Delayed hemolytic
- Posttransfusion graft-versus-host disease
- Noncardiac pulmonary edema

Types of Blood Products

- Red blood cells (RBCs)
  — Packed RBCs (PRBCs)
  — Autologous PRBCs
  — Washed RBCs
  — Frozen RBCs
  — Leukocyte-poor RBCs
  — RBC units with high number of reticulocytes (young RBCs)
- Other cellular components
  — Platelets
  — Granulocytes
- Plasma components
  — Fresh frozen plasma (FFP)
  — Cryoprecipitate
  — Serum albumin
  — Plasma protein fraction (PPF)
  — Immune serum globulin

Nursing Interventions

- Assessment before, during, and after the transfusion including the IV site
- Confirm informed consent
- Identify the compatibility
- Initiation of a transfusion slowly then maintain the infusion rate
  — 1 unit of packed RBCs is transfused in 2 to 4 hr.

A client who is receiving a transfusion of packed red blood cells has an inflamed IV site. What action should the nurse implement?

A. Double-check the blood type of the unit of blood transfusing with another nurse.

B. Discontinue the transfusion and send the remaining blood and tubing to the lab.

C. Immediately start a new IV at another site and resume the transfusion at the new site.

D. Continue to monitor the site for signs of infection and notify the healthcare provider.

HESI Hint

Be able to prioritize what to do first if client exhibits S/S of transfusion reaction

- **STOP THE TRANSFUSION**
- Maintain IV line with NS
- Check vital signs
- Notify physician immediately
- Treat shock or anaphylaxis
- Send blood and urine specimens to lab
- Send blood and tubing to lab

1. Is the item written in a positive or a negative style?

2. Find the key words in the question.

3. Rephrase the question in your own words.

4. Rule out options:
   -
   -
   -

Disseminated Intravascular Coagulation (DIC)

- DIC is an abnormal response of the normal clotting cascade stimulated by a disease process or disorder.
  - DIC results from abnormally initiated and accelerated clotting.
  - Subsequent decreases in clotting factors and platelets ensue.
  - May lead to uncontrollable hemorrhage
- As more clots are made, more breakdown products from fibrinogen and fibrin are also formed. They work in three ways to interfere with blood coagulation.
  - Coat the platelets and interfere with platelet function
  - Interfere with thrombin and thereby disrupt coagulation
  - Attach to fibrinogen, which interferes with the process necessary to form a clot
- D-Dimer assay test measures the degree of fibrinolysis.
- Appropriate nursing interventions are essential to the survival of the client.
  - Astute, ongoing assessment
    - Early detection of bleeding, both occult and overt, must be a primary goal.
    - The patient is assessed for signs of external and internal bleeding.
  - Active attention to manifestations of the syndrome
  - Institution of appropriate treatment measures, which can be challenging and sometimes paradoxic
    - Heparin infusion

Acute Respiratory Distress Syndrome (ARDS)

- ARDS is considered to be present if the client has the following:
  - Refractory hypoxemia
  - Chest x-ray with new bilateral interstitial or alveolar infiltrates
    - The chest x-ray is often termed whiteout or white lung.
  - Pulmonary artery wedge pressure of 18 mm Hg or less and no evidence of heart failure
  - A predisposing condition for ARDS within 48 hours of clinical manifestations
  - Alveolar capillary membrane damage with subsequent leakage of fluids into the interstitial spaces and the alveoli
- As ARDS progresses, it is associated with profound respiratory distress requiring endotracheal intubation and PPV.

Nursing Assessment

- Dyspnea
- Scattered crackles
- Intercostal retractions
- Pink frothy sputum
- Cyanosis
- Hypoxemia
- Hypercapnia
- Respiratory acidosis

Nursing Diagnoses

- Impaired Gas Exchange
  — Related to ↓ V/Q perfusion ratio
- Ineffective Airway Clearance
  — Related to ↑ secretions
- Decreased Cardiac Output
  — Related to ↓ venous return

Nursing Plans and Interventions

- The overall goals for the patient with ARDS
  — PaO_2 of at least 60 mm Hg
  — Adequate lung ventilation to maintain normal pH
- The goals for a patient recovering from ARDS
  — PaO_2 within normal limits for age or baseline values on room air
  — SaO_2 greater than 90%
  — Patent airway
  — Clear lungs on auscultation
- Positive end-expiratory pressure (PEEP)
  — This ventilatory option creates positive pressure at end exhalation and restores functional residual capacity (FRC).

Life Support
CPR

- Cardiac arrest is the *most common* event requiring CPR

CPR and Choking Basics (Adults)

- Establish an airway
- Ventilate with 2 breaths
- Maintain circulation
- Perform CPR
  — 30:2 ratio of compression/ventilation
  — 100 compressions/min
- DO NOT try to intervene if choking person CAN speak, cough, or breathe

CPR and Choking Basics (Neonates and Children 1 to 8)

- Most common indications for CPR in children are NOT the same as for adults.
  — Neonates and infants: hypoxia, hypoglycemia, hypothermia, acidosis, hypercoagulability
  — Children: respiratory arrest, prolonged hypoxemia secondary to respiratory insult or shock, including septic shock
- Guidelines vary based on age of child.
  — Ventilation technique and rate
  — Compression technique and rate
  — How to manage the obstructed airway

HESI Hint

- NCLEX questions focus on common symptoms.
  — Chest pain
- NCLEX-RN questions will focus on basic CPR.
  — Basics of CPR are all that are required to begin practice.

A client in shock develops a central venous pressure (CVP) of 2 cm of water and a mean arterial pressure (MAP) of 60 mm Hg. Which prescribed intervention should the nurse implement first?

A. Increase the rate of O_2 flow
B. Obtain arterial blood gas results
C. Insert an indwelling urinary catheter
D. Increase the rate of IV fluids

1. Is the item written in a positive or a negative style?

2. Find the key words in the question.

3. Rephrase the question in your own words.

4. Rule out options:
    ■
    ■
    ■

Cardiac Monitoring

■ A standard ECG uses 12 leads.
    — Provides *best* overall evaluation
■ Telemetry
    — Usually 3 leads show one view of the heart
■ Holter monitor
    — Usually on for 24-hour continuous reading
■ P wave
    — Atrial depolarization

Electrocardiogram (ECG)

■ QRS complex
    — Ventricular depolarization
    — Normal <0.11 second
■ ST segment
    — Early ventricular repolarization
■ PR interval
    — Time for impulse to travel through SA node
    — Normal 0.12 to 0.2 second
■ R-R interval
    — Measure regularity of heartbeat

HESI Hint
REMEMBER!!
■ *Always* treat the patient, NOT the MONITOR.
■ NCLEX-RN questions will relate to early recognition of symptoms and early intervention.
■ DO NOT be tricked into choosing an intervention if the patient otherwise appears stable.

Which assignment should the nurse delegate to an unlicensed assistive personnel (UAP) in an acute care setting?

A. Hourly blood glucose checks for a client with a continuous insulin drip
B. Giving PO medications left at the bedside for the client to take after eating
C. Taking vital signs for an older client with left humerus and left tibial fractures
D. Replacing a client's decubitus dressing soiled from incontinence

1. Is the item written in a positive or a negative style?

2. Find the key words in the question.

3. Rephrase the question in your own words.

4. Rule out options:
    ■
    ■
    ■

5 Medical-Surgical Nursing

RESPIRATORY SYSTEM

A male client who is 1 day postoperative after a left pneumonectomy is lying on his right side with the head of bed (HOB) elevated 10 degrees. The nurse assesses his respiratory rate at 32/min. What action should the nurse implement first?
A. Elevate the head of the bed
B. Assist to supine position
C. Measure O_2 saturation
D. Administer PRN morphine IV

1. Is the item written in a positive or a negative style?

2. Find the key words in the question.

3. Rephrase the question in your own words.

4. Rule out options:
   ■
   ■
   ■

Pneumonia Pathophysiology
Pneumonia results in inflammation of lung tissue causing consolidation of exudate.
- Pathogens
  — Bacterial (gram-negative most severe), viral (rare), fungal
- Host's physical status
  — Aspiration
  — Inhalation
  — Hypostatic
- Anatomical areas
  — Lung parenchyma
  — Pleurae

Classification
Classification depends on where the infection was acquired.
- Community-acquired pneumonia (CAP)
  — With the rise in the elderly population, an increasingly important form of CAP is nursing home–acquired pneumonia (NHAP).
- Hospital-acquired pneumonia (HAP)
  — HAP, also referred to as nosocomial pneumonia, includes the subset of ventilator-associated pneumonia (VAP).

Nursing Assessment
- Tachypnea
- Fever—abrupt onset
- Dyspnea
- Cyanosis
- Mental status changes
- Crackles, decreased breath sounds
- Dullness with percussion

Diagnostic Tests

- Chest x-ray
- Sputum Gram stain (culture and sensitivity if drug resistant)
- Blood gases
- Complete blood cell count (CBC)
- Pulse oximetry and/or arterial blood gases (ABGs)
- Cold agglutinins and complement fixation studies
- Thoracentesis

Nursing Plans and Interventions

- Hand washing to reduce cross contamination
- Antibiotics
- Isolation if prescribed
- Administer fluids
- Manage pain
- Monitor oxygenation (humidified to loosen secretions)

Anti-infective Medications

- Penicillins
  — Semisynthetic penicillins
    • Oxacillin
  — Anti-pseudomonal penicillins
    • Ampicillin
- Tetracyclines
  — Doxycycline hyclate (Vibramycin)
- Aminoglycosides
  — Gentamicin sulfate
- Cephalosporins
  — Ceftriaxone (Rocephin)
- Macrolides
  — Clarithromycin (Biaxin)
- Fluoroquinolones
  — Ciprofloxacin (Cipro)

Chronic Airflow Limitation (CAL)
Chronic Obstructive Pulmonary Disease (COPD)

- Emphysema and chronic bronchitis
  — Chronic progressive disease
- Asthma
  — Reversible disease

Chronic Bronchitis

- Pathophysiology
  — Chronic sputum with cough production on a daily basis for a minimum of 3 months/year
  — Chronic hypoxemia/cor pulmonale
  — Increase in mucus, cilia production
  — Increase in bronchial wall thickness (obstructs air flow)
- Exacerbations usually due to infection
- Increased V/Q abnormalities
- Increased CO_2 retention/acidemia
- Increased pulmonary artery pressure (PAP) = cor pulmonale
- Reduced responsiveness of respiratory center to hypoxemic stimuli

"Blue Bloaters"

- Generalized cyanosis
- Right-sided heart failure
  — Peripheral edema
- Productive cough

Emphysema

- Abnormal enlargement of the air spaces distal to the terminal alveolar walls
- Increased dyspnea/work of breathing
  — Reduced gas exchange surface area
  — Increased air trapping (increased anterior-posterior diameter)
  — Decreased capillary network
  — Increased work/increased O_2 consumption

"Pink Puffers"

- Barrel chest
- Thin
- Noncyanotic
- Pursed-lip breather

COPD Etiology/Precipitating Factors

- Cigarette smoking
- Environmental/occupational exposure
- Genetic predisposition

COPD Assessment Data

- Inspection
  — Bronchitis
    - Right-sided heart failure
    - Cyanosis ("blue bloaters")
    - Distended neck veins
  — Emphysema
    - Pursed-lip breathing
    - "Pink puffer"
- Auscultation
  — Bronchitis
    - Crackles
    - Rhonchi
    - Expiratory wheezes
  — Emphysema
    - Distant breath sounds
    - Quiet breath sounds
    - Wheezes

COPD Diagnostic Findings

- Hypoxemia
- Hypercapnia
- Polycythemia
- Reduced expiratory flow
- Pulmonary blebs on x-ray (emphysema)

COPD Nursing Plans and Interventions

- Lowest O_2 to prevent CO_2 retention
  — Respiratory drive based on O_2 levels
- Monitor for signs and symptoms (S/S) of fluid overload
- Baseline ABGs for CO_2 retainers
- Client teaching—pursed-lip breathing
- Orthopneic position

Reactive Airway Disease
Asthma/status asthmaticus

Inflammatory disorder of the airways that is characterized by an exaggerated bronchoconstrictor response to a wide variety of stimuli
- Allergens
- Environmental irritants
- Cold air
- Exercise
- Beta blockers
- Respiratory infection
- Emotional stress
- Reflux esophagitis

Bronchodilators
- Adrenergics
- Sympathomimetics
- Methylxanthine
- Corticosteroids
- Anticholinergics

Nursing Assessment
- Dyspnea, wheezing, chest tightness
- Assess precipitating factors
- Medication history

Nursing Interventions
- Monitor respirations and assess breath sounds
- Monitor oxygen saturation (ABGs or pulse oximetry)
- Monitor mental status
- Chest physiotherapy
- Assess peripheral pulses and warmth and color of extremities
- Position for maximum ventilation
- Encourage slow, pursed-lip breathing.
- Encourage abdominal breathing and abdominal muscle exercises
- Administer humidified oxygen therapy as prescribed

The nurse palpates a crackling sensation of the skin around the chest tube insertion site of a client after thoracic surgery. What action should the nurse implement?
A. Return to surgery
B. Prepare for insertion of a larger chest tube
C. Increase the water-seal suction pressure
D. Continue to monitor

Head and Neck Cancer
- Typically squamous cell in origin.
- Tumor sites
  — Paranasal sinuses
  — Oral cavity
  — Nasopharynx
  — Oropharynx
  — Larynx

1. Is the item written in a positive or a negative style?

2. Find the key words in the question.

3. Rephrase the question in your own words.

4. Rule out options:
   -
   -
   -

- Disability is great because of the potential loss of voice, disfigurement, and social consequences.
- Head and neck cancer is most common in males over the age of 50 and is related to heavy tobacco and alcohol intake.

Cancer of the Larynx
Nursing Assessment
- Hoarseness of the voice
- Change in vocal cord quality
- Dysphagia
- Dyspnea
- Neck pain radiating to ear
- Sensation of a lump in the throat

Surgery
Partial laryngectomy
- Hemilaryngectomy
  — Hoarse voice
  — Initially need swallowing therapy to learn how to swallow without aspirating
- Supraglottic partial laryngectomy
  — Normal voice
  — Initially need swallowing therapy to learn how to swallow without aspirating

Total laryngectomy
- No voice
- No swallowing problem

Nursing Plans and Care
- Preoperative teaching
  — Explain suctioning
  — Plan method of communication
  — Refer to speech pathologist
- Postoperative care
  — Monitor for bleeding, airway obstruction
  — Subcutaneous emphysema
  — S/S of infection
  — Assess respiratory status every 1 to 2 hours

Tuberculosis (TB)
TB is an infectious disease caused by the bacillus *Mycobacterium tuberculosis* or the tubercle bacillus, an acid-fast organism.

Resurgence of TB in the United States
- Related to HIV infection
- Multidrug-resistant TB (MDR-TB)
  — Rifampin
  — Isoniazid
- Seen disproportionately in poor, underserved, and minorities

Nursing Assessment

- Low-grade fever
- Pallor
- Chills
- Night sweats
- Easy fatigability
- Anorexia
- Weight loss

Nursing Interventions

- Respiratory isolation
- Medication regimen
  — Isoniazid (INH therapy)
  — Pyridoxine (vitamin B$_6$)
  — Rifampin (Rifadin)
  — Pyrazinamide
  — Take as prescribed 9 to 12 months
  — Teach side effects

Lung Cancer

- Number one cancer in the United States!
- The increase in death rates for both men and women is directly related to cigarette smoking.

Nursing Assessment

- Symptoms of lung cancer are not usually apparent until the disease is in the advanced stages.
- Persistent hacking cough may be either dry or productive with blood-tinged sputum.
- Hoarseness
- Dyspnea
- Abnormal chest x-ray
- Positive sputum on cytological exam

Treatment

- Chemotherapy
- Radiation therapy
- Surgical intervention
  — Pneumonectomy—removal of entire lung
  — Lobectomy—segmental resection
- Nursing care depends upon the type of medical treatment prescribed.

Immediate Postoperative Care

- Promote ventilation and reexpansion of the lung by:
  — Maintaining a clear airway
  — Maintaining the closed drainage system if one is used
    • Promoting arm exercises to maintain full use on the operated side
    • Promoting nutrition
    • Monitoring the incision for bleeding and subcutaneous emphysema

HESI Hints
Skills to Review

- Tracheal care and suctioning
- Ventilator setting maintenance
- Oxygen administration
- Pulse oximetry
- Respiratory isolation techniques
- Proper use of inhalers
- Teach pursed-lip breathing

A client who has acute renal failure is admitted and the potassium level is 6.4 mEq/L. Which snack should the nurse offer?
A. An orange
B. A milk shake
C. Dried fruit and nuts
D. A gelatin dessert

Acute Renal Failure (ARF)
- A reversible syndrome if symptoms are caught early enough!
- Remember:
  — Kidneys use 25% of normal cardiac output to maintain function.
  — Kidneys excrete 1 to 2 L of urine per 24 hours for adults.
  — Three types of ARF
    - Prerenal
    - Intrarenal
    - Postrenal

Prerenal Failure
- Etiological factors
  — Hemorrhage
  — Hypovolemia
  — Decreased cardiac output
  — Decreased renal perfusion

Intrarenal Failure
- Etiological factors
  — May develop secondary to prerenal failure
  — Nephrotoxins
  — Infections (glomerulonephritis)
  — Renal injury
  — Vascular lesions

Postrenal Failure
- Etiological factors for obstruction
  — Calculi
  — Benign prostatic hyperplasia (BPH)
  — Tumors
  — Strictures

Nursing Assessment
- Decreased urine output
- Weight gain
- Edema
- Diagnostic test results: oliguric phase
  — ↓ Urine output
  — ↑ BUN (blood urea nitrogen) and creatinine
  — ↑ Potassium
  — ↓ Sodium (serum)

1. Is the item written in a positive or a negative style?

2. Find the key words in the question.

3. Rephrase the question in your own words.

4. Rule out options:
   -
   -
   -

— ↓ pH
— Metabolic acidosis
— ↑ Urine sodium
— Fixed at 1.010, specific gravity
■ Diagnostic test results: diuretic phase
— ↑ Urine output
— ↓ Fluid volume
— ↓ Potassium
— ↓ Sodium
— ↓ Urine specific gravity
— ↓ Urine sodium

Nursing Plans and Interventions
■ In oliguric phase give only enough fluids to replace losses + 400 to 500 mL/24 hr
■ Strict I & O
■ Monitor lab values closely
■ Watch for ECG changes
■ Monitor weight daily

After hemodialysis, the nurse is evaluating the blood results for a client who has end-stage renal disease. Which value should the nurse verify with the laboratory?
A. Elevated serum potassium
B. Increase in serum calcium
C. Low hemoglobin
D. Reduction in serum sodium

Chronic Kidney Disease (CKD)
■ End-stage renal disease
■ Progressive irreversible damage to the nephrons and glomeruli
■ Causes
— Diabetic nephropathy
— Hypertensive nephrosclerosis
— Glomerulonephritis
— Polycystic kidney disease

Nursing Assessment
■ Early stage
— Polyuria
— Renal insufficiency
■ Late stage
— Oliguria
— Hematuria

HESI Hint
■ Body weight good indicator of fluid retention
■ Watch for hyperkalemia
■ Assess level of consciousness (LOC)
■ Limit high-potassium foods
■ Watch protein intake

Be Prepared for NCLEX-RN Questions
■ Be able to recognize foods that would be inappropriate for ARF client
■ Abnormal lab values:
— Hyperkalemia
— Hyponatremia
■ Symptoms of fluid volume excess

1. **Is the item written in a positive or a negative style?**

2. **Find the key words in the question.**

3. **Rephrase the question in your own words.**

4. **Rule out options:**
   ■
   ■
   ■

- Proteinuria
- Edema
- Increased BP
- Muscle wasting, secondary to negative nitrogen balance
- Ammonia taste in mouth
- $\uparrow$ Creatinine, $\uparrow$ phosphorus, $\uparrow$ potassium
■ End stage
- Anuria (<100 mL/24 hr)

Nursing Plans and Interventions

■ Monitor serum electrolytes
■ Weigh daily
■ Strict I & O
■ Renal diet
- Low protein
- Low sodium
- Low potassium
- Low phosphate

Medications

■ Drugs to manage the associated complications
- Aluminum hydroxide (to bind phosphates)
- Epoetin (Epogen) (to treat anemia)
- Antihypertensive therapy
- Calcium supplements and vitamin D
- Antihyperlipidemics
- Statins (to lower LDL)
- Fibrates (to lower triglycerides)
■ CAUTION: As kidney function decreases, medication doses need adjustment.

Renal Dialysis

■ Hemodialysis
- AV fistula
■ Ø Venipunctures, Ø IVs, Ø BP in AV shunt arm
■ Withhold medications that would affect hemodynamic stability prior to dialysis
■ Continuous hemofiltration
- Requires vascular access, used in special care units
■ Peritoneal dialysis
- Monitor indwell and outflow times closely
- Monitor I & O

Postoperative Care: Kidney Surgery

■ Respiratory status
- Auscultate to detect "wet" sounds
- Demonstrate splinting method
■ Circulatory status
- Monitor for shock
- Monitor surgical site for bleeding
■ Pain relief status
- Administer narcotic analgesics as needed
■ Urinary status
- Check urinary output and drainage from ALL tubes
- Strict I & O

HESI Hint

■ Be alert for Digoxin toxicity
- Digoxin is excreted by kidneys
- S/S: N/V, arrhythmias, heart rate <60 beats/min
■ Keep calorie intake high to ensure protein is spared
- Hard candies, jelly beans, flavored CHO powders are used
■ Watch for hyperglycemia in clients getting peritoneal dialysis

A client with a 20-year history of type 1 diabetes mellitus is having renal function tests because of recent fatigue, weakness, a blood urea nitrogen (BUN) of 24 mg/dL, and serum creatinine of 1.6 mg/dL. What further inquiry should the nurse make related to early symptoms of renal insufficiency?

A. Dyspnea
B. Nocturia
C. Confusion
D. Stomatitis

1. Is the item written in a positive or a negative style?

2. Find the key words in the question.

3. Rephrase the question in your own words.

4. Rule out options:
   ■
   ■
   ■

Urinary Tract Infections

■ Obtain clean-catch midstream specimen
■ Administer antibiotics as ordered
  — Take fully prescribed dose
  — Don't skip doses
■ Encourage fluid intake of 3000 mL per day
■ Encourage voiding every 2 to 3 hours

Urinary Tract Obstruction

■ Caused by calculi or stones
■ Location of pain can help locate stone
  — Flank pain (stone usually in upper ureter)
  — Pain radiating to abdomen (stone likely in ureter or bladder)
■ Nursing plan
  — Administer narcotics
  — Strain all urine
  — Encourage high fluid intake
    • 3 to 4 L per day
  — Strict I & O
  — May need surgical management

Benign Prostatic Hyperplasia

■ Enlargement of the prostrate
  — Most common treatment: transurethral resection of the prostate (TURP)
  — Can be done with laser to burn out prostate
  — If prostate is too large will use suprapubic approach
  — Assess for
    • Increased urinary frequency/decreased output
    • Bladder distention (increases risk of spasm)

Nursing Plans and Interventions

■ Preoperative teaching
  — Pain management
  — Oversized balloon catheter
■ Bladder spasms
  — Common after surgery
  — Use antispasmodics
    • Belladonna and opium suppositories
    • Ditropan
    • Bentyl

- Continuous bladder irrigation is typically done to remove blood clots and ensure drainage
- Drainage should be reddish pink for 24 hours, clearing to light pink
- Monitor color and amount of urine output
- Notify physician if client has bright red bleeding with large clots

Discharge Teaching
- Continue to drink 12 to 14 glasses of water per day
- Avoid straining
- Avoid strenuous activity, sports, lifting, and intercourse for 3 to 4 weeks
- Report large amounts of blood or frank blood

The charge nurse is making assignments on the renal unit. Which client should the nurse assign to an LPN who is new to the unit?
A. An older client who is draining thick, dark, red drainage in a urinary catheter 1 day after a transurethral prostatic resection
B. A middle-aged client admitted with acute renal failure secondary to reaction to IVP dye
C. A older client who has end-stage renal disease and complains of nausea after receiving Lanoxin
D. A middle-aged client who receives hemodialysis and is prescribed epoetin (Epogen) subcutaneous daily

CARDIOVASCULAR SYSTEM

The nurse is administering 0900 medications to three clients on a telemetry unit when the unlicensed assistive personnel (UAP) reports that another client is complaining of a sudden onset of substernal discomfort. What action should the nurse implement?
A. Ask the UAP to obtain the client's VS
B. Assess the client's discomfort
C. Advise the client to rest in bed
D. Observe the client's ECG pattern

Coronary Artery Disease (CAD)
- Prevalent etiologies of CAD
  — Atherosclerosis
    • Partially or completely blocked coronary arteries
  — Coronary vasospasm
  — Microvascular angina
- CAD results in ischemia and infarction of myocardial tissue
- LAD (left anterior descending artery) most commonly affected
- CAD remains the number one health problem in the United States

1. Is the item written in a positive or a negative style?

2. Find the key words in the question.

3. Rephrase the question in your own words.

4. Rule out options:
   ■
   ■
   ■

1. Is the item written in a positive or a negative style?

2. Find the key words in the question.

3. Rephrase the question in your own words.

4. Rule out options:
   ■
   ■
   ■

Angina

- Varies from mild to severe, transient to prolonged, gradual or sudden onset
- May radiate to either arm, shoulder, jaw, neck, or epigastric area
- Other S/S: dyspnea, tachycardia, palpitations, nausea and vomiting, fatigue, diaphoresis, pallor, syncope
- Usually subsides with rest or nitroglycerin
- Often precipitated by exercise, cold exposure, heavy meal, stress, intercourse

Reduction of Risk Factors

- Stop smoking
- Lose weight
- Decrease blood pressure
- Increase activity/exercise

Diet Therapy

- Diet modification
- Goal is to reduce serum cholesterol and serum triglycerides
- Maintain ideal body weight
- Daily cholesterol intake should be restricted to <200 mg/day

Drug Therapy

- May be initiated if diet modification unsuccessful
- Antiplatelet
  — Acetylsalicylic acid (ASA)
  — Clopidogrel (Plavix)
- Beta blockers
- Atenolol (Tenormin)
- Metoprolol (Lopressor, Toprol)
- Nitrates
  — Nitroglycerin
  — Nitroprusside
- Calcium channel blockers
  — Diltiazem (Cardizem)
  — Verapamil (Calan, Isoptin)
- Thrombolytics
  — Alteplase (recombinant t-PA) (Activase)
  — Reteplase (r-PA) (Retavase)
  — Tenecteplase (TNK-tPA)
  — Streptokinase (Streptase)
- Anticoagulants
  — Unfractionated heparin
  — Low-molecular-weight heparin (LMWH) (enoxaparin [Lovenox])
- Angiotensin-converting enzyme inhibitors
  — Captopril (Capoten)
  — Enalapril (Vasotec)
  — Benazepril (Lotensin)
- Analgesics
  — Morphine sulfate

NCLEX QUESTION FOCUS

- Picking out probable risk factors
- Choose modifying behaviors
- Education!

Cholesterol-Lowering Drugs

- May be initiated if diet modification unsuccessful
  - Atorvastatin (Lipitor)
  - Lovastatin (Mevacor)
  - Pravastatin (Pravachol)
  - Rosuvastatin (Crestor)
  - Simvastatin (Zocor)
  - Ezetemibe (Zetia)
  - Gemfibrozil (Lopid)
  - Niacin (nicotinic acid)

Oxygen

- Administer at 4-6 L/min to assist in oxygenating myocardial tissue

Nitroglycerin

- Dilates the coronary arteries
- Increases blood flow to the damaged area of myocardium
- Dose:
  - 0.4 mg/tablet
  - 1 tab sublingual q 5 min × 3 doses

Morphine Sulfate

- Analgesic
- ↓ Anxiety
- ↓ Tachypnea
- Relaxes bronchial smooth muscle
- Improves gas exchange

Thrombolytic Therapy

- Useful when infarction is diagnosed early
- Streptokinase and tPA
  - Administered IV
  - Most effective if given within 6 hours of onset of chest pain
- Heparin therapy will usually follow thrombolytic therapy

Beta Blockers

- Decrease heart rate
- Reduce workload of heart
- Decrease oxygen demand of myocardium

Calcium Channel Blockers

- Decrease conduction through AV node
- Slows heart rate
- Decrease oxygen demand by myocardium

Medical Interventions

- Percutaneous transluminal coronary angioplasty (PTCA)
  - Balloon angioplasty
- Intracoronary stents
- Less commonly used percutaneous coronary interventions procedures
  - Directional coronary atherectomy
  - Laser therapy
  - Transluminal extraction catheterization
  - Rotablation

- Transmyocardial laser revascularization
- Coronary artery bypass graft (CABG)

Acute Myocardial Infarction
- Destruction of myocardial tissue due to lack of blood and oxygen supply
- Begins with an occlusion of coronary artery
- Ischemia, injury, infarction

Ischemia
- Results from reduced blood flow and oxygen to the coronary arteries
- If not reversed, then injury occurs
- Ischemia lasting 20 minutes or more is sufficient to produce irreversible tissue damage

Injury
- Prolonged interruption of oxygen supply and nutrients
- Cells are still salvageable

Infarction
- Tissue necrosis and death
- Irreversible damage
- Scar tissue: has no electrical stimulation or contractility
- Within 24 hours of infarction the healing process begins

Complications
- Up to 90% of clients suffer complications, including
  — Dysrhythmias
  — Cardiac failure
  — Cardiogenic shock
  — Thromboembolism
  — Ventricular rupture

Signs and Symptoms
- Pain
  — Sudden onset—severity increases
  — May persist for hours or days—not relieved by rest or nitroglycerine
  — Heavy/constrictive
  — Located behind the sternum
  — May radiate to arms, back, neck, or jaw
- Skin: cool and clammy
- Rapid, irregular, feeble pulse

Atypical Symptoms
- Women
  — Discomfort rather than pain
  — Shortness of breath
  — Extreme fatigue
- Diabetics
  — Asymptomatic
  — Neuropathy
  — Dyspnea
- Geriatrics
  — Confusion
  — Change in mental status
  — Dizziness
  — Shortness of breath

HESI Hint
Not all clients have pain (e.g., those with diabetic neuropathy)

Medical Diagnosis

Confirm by diagnostics

- ECG (12 lead)
- Confirm by lab tests
- Troponin
- Myoglobin
- Cardiac enzymes

Cardiac Lab Tests

- Troponin:
  - Found only in cardiac muscle
  - May present as early as 1 hr after injury
  - Peaks within 24 hours
  - Returns to normal in 5-14 days
- Myoglobin:
  - Released 1 hour after an acute myocardial infarction (MI)
  - Rises before creatine kinase-MB levels
  - Returns to normal within 24 hours
- Cardiac enzymes
  - With sustained ischemia, enzymes are released into the interstitial fluid
  - Are assessed at regular intervals to confirm acute MI

A client complains of a severe headache after receiving nitroglycerin 0.4 mg SL for angina. What prescription should the nurse administer?

A. A second dose of nitroglycerin
B. A scheduled dose of low-dose aspirin
C. A PRN dose of acetaminophen PO
D. A PRN dose of morphine sulfate IV

1. Is the item written in a positive or a negative style?

2. Find the key words in the question.

3. Rephrase the question in your own words.

4. Rule out options:
   -
   -
   -

Treatment

- Overall goal is to preserve myocardial tissue
- Drug therapy
  - Oxygen
  - Nitroglycerine
  - Morphine
  - Thrombolytic therapy
  - Other meds
- Angioplasty and stents
  - Used when drug therapy is not successful
- Coronary artery bypass graft
  - Severe coronary artery disease detected
  - Can be emergent or elective

What to Do When a Client Complains of Chest Pain

- Assess pain
  - 1-10 scale, Wong-Baker FACES scale
  - Duration, description, type
- Check vital signs and O_2 saturation, apply oxygen

- Notify physician
- ECG
- Cardiac enzymes
- Administer aspirin, nitroglycerin, morphine sulfate

The nurse is planning a class on stroke prevention for clients with hypertension. What information is most important to provide the clients in the class?

A. Salt restriction diet
B. Weight reduction
C. Medication compliance
D. Risk for stroke

Hypertension (HTN)

- Persistent BP elevation >140/90 mm Hg
- Risk factors:
  — Nonmodifiable: family history, gender, age, ethnicity
  — Modifiable: use of alcohol, tobacco, caffeine; sedentary lifestyle; obesity

HTN Education

- Number one cause of stroke (cerebrovascular accident, CVA) is noncompliance with HTN medications.

Medications

- Diuretics
  — Thiazides—Zaroxolyn
- Antihypertensives
  — Minipress, Corgard, Tenormin, Catapres
- ACE inhibitors
  — Zestril
- Calcium channel blockers
  — Cardizem

Peripheral Vascular Disease
Arterial

- Smooth shiny skin
- Pallor on elevation
- Weak peripheral pulses
- Sharp or tingling pain
- Cool to touch
- Intermittent claudication (classic symptom)
- Painful, nonedematous ulcers

Venous

- Monitor for history of deep vein thrombosis
- Bluish purple skin discoloration
- Normal peripheral pulses
- Warm to touch
- Slightly painful ulcers with marked edema

1. Is the item written in a positive or a negative style?

2. Find the key words in the question.

3. Rephrase the question in your own words.

4. Rule out options:
   -
   -
   -

NCLEX QUESTION FOCUS

- Picking out probable risk factors and choosing modifying behaviors
- Education!

Nursing Interventions and Treatment

General

- Change positions frequently; avoid sitting with crossed legs
- Wear NO restrictive clothing
- Keep extremities warm with clothing, not external heaters
- Discourage smoking
- Thrombolytic agents if thrombosis

Arterial

- Bed rest
- Topical antibiotics
- Surgical intervention

Venous

- Systemic antibiotics
- Compression dressing
- Limb elevation

Abdominal Aortic Aneurysm

- Pulsating abdominal mass
- Bruit heard over abdomen
- Confirmed on x-ray
- If ruptures: S/S of hypovolemic shock
- Surgical repair of aneurysm—postop care
  - Monitor for S/S of renal failure, postop ileus
  - Changes in pulses, S/S of occluded graft

Types of Aneurysms

- Fusiform
- Saccular
- Mycotic
  - Staphylococci
  - Streptococci
  - Salmonellae
- Pseudoaneurysms

Thrombophlebitis

- Inflammation of the venous wall with clot formation
- S/S: calf pain, + Homans' sign, edema of calf
- Restrict ambulation
- Elevate extremity
- Antiembolic stockings
- Medications
  - Heparin therapy
    - Monitor partial thromboplastin time (PTT)
  - Coumadin therapy
    - Monitor prothrombin time (PT), international normalized ratio (INR)
  - Antiplatelet agents
    - Ticlid
    - Plavix

Dysrhythmias

- Client may be asymptomatic until cardiac output is altered
- May complain of palpitations, syncope, pain, dyspnea, diaphoresis

- Will display change in pulse rate/rhythm and ECG changes
- Always treat the client and NOT the monitor!

Atrial Dysrhythmias
- A-fib (atrial fibrillation)
  — Chaotic activity in the AV node
  — No true P waves visible
  — Irregular ventricular rhythm
  — Risk for CVA
  Anticoagulant therapy is needed
- Atrial flutter
  — Sawtoothed waveform
  — Fluttering in chest
  — Ventricular rhythm states regular
- May use cardioversion to treat either atrial dysrhythmia

Ventricular Dysrhythmias
- V-tach (ventricular tachycardia)
  — Wide bizarre QRS complex
  — Assess whether patient has a pulse
  — Is cardiac output impaired?
  — Prepare for synchronized cardioversion
  — Administer antiarrhythmic drugs
- V-fib (ventricular fibrillation)
  — Cardiac emergency
  — No cardiac output
  — Start cardiopulmonary resuscitation (CPR)
  — Defibrillate as quickly as possible
  — Administer antiarrhythmic drugs

Antiarrhythmic Medications
- Class I: sodium channel blockers (decrease conduction velocity in the atria, ventricles, and His-Purkinje system)
  IA
  — Disopyramide (Norpace)
  — Procainamide (Pronestyl)
  — Quinidine
  IB
  — Lidocaine (Xylocaine)
  — Mexiletine (Mexitil)
  — Phenytoin (Dilantin)
  — Tocainide (Tonocard)
  IC
  — Flecainide (Tambocor)
  — Propafenone (Rythmol)
  Other Class I
  — Moricizine (Ethmozine)
- Class II: β-adrenergic blockers (decrease automaticity of the SA node, decrease conduction velocity in AV node)
  — Acebutolol (Sectral)
  — Atenolol (Tenormin)
  — Esmolol (Brevibloc)
  — Metoprolol (Lopressor)
  — Sotalol (Betapace)

- Class III: potassium channel blockers (delay repolarization)
  — Amiodarone (Cordarone)
  — Dofetilide (Tikosyn)
  — Sotalol (Betapace)
- Class IV: calcium channel blockers (decrease automaticity of SA node, delay AV node conduction)
  — Diltiazem (Cardizem)
  — Verapamil (Calan)
- Other antidysrhythmic drugs
  — Adenosine (Adenocard)
  — Digoxin (Lanoxin)
  — Ibutilide (Corvert)
  — Magnesium

Heart Failure
Etiology
- Coronary artery disease (CAD), prior MI
- Chronic HTN
- Cardiomyopathy
  — Dilated
- Idiopathic
- Thyroid
- Diabetes
  — Restrictive
  — Ischemic
- Valvular and congenital heart disease
- Pulmonary diseases

Left-Sided Heart Failure (LHF)
- Causes: LV infarct, cardiomyopathy
- Symptoms: dyspnea, cough, fluid accumulation in lungs
- Signs: S_3 gallop, tachycardia, inspiratory rales beginning at lung bases, expiratory wheezes due to bronchospasms (misdiagnosed with asthma)
- Laboratory findings: ABGs reveal hypoxemia, chest x-ray shows pulmonary edema or pleural effusions

Right-Sided Heart Failure (RHF)— Systemic Congestion
- Causes: LHF, RV infarct, pulmonary or tricuspid valve disease, pulmonary HTN, COPD, PE
- Symptoms: dyspnea on exertion, fatigue, weight gain, fluid retention
- Signs: increased central venous pressure (CVP), jugular venous distention (JVD) >3-4 cm, hepatomegaly, ascites, peripheral or sacral edema, pleural and pericardial effusions are also not uncommon

RHF laboratory tests
- Liver function shows hepatic congestion
- Increased liver enzymes, increased PT, INR
- Hyponatremia (fluid restriction only if Na^+ <132 mg/dL
- Increased BUN/creatinine = decreased renal perfusion

Sodium and volume homeostasis
- As CO decreases, renal perfusion decreases.
- This activates the renin-angiotensin system.
- This causes fluid retention.

Pharmacological Management

- Angiotensin-converting enzyme (ACE) inhibitors
  — Captopril
  — Enalapril
  — Fosinopril
  — Lisinopril
  — Quinapril
  — Ramipril
  — Perindopril
  — Benazepril
- Diuretics
- Loop diuretics
  — Furosemide
  — Bumetanide
  — Torsemide
- Thiazides
  — Thiazide-related drug: metolazone
- Aldosterone antagonists
  — Spironolactone
  — Eplerenone
- Inotropes
  — Digoxin
  — Dobutamine
- Phosphodiesterase inhibitors
  — Milrinone
- Natriuretic peptides
  — Nesiritide
- Beta blockers
  — Metoprolol
  — Carvedilol
  — Bisoprolol
- Angiotensin II receptor blockers
  — Losartan
  — Candesartan
  — Valsartan
- Vasodilators
  — Nitrates: isosorbide dinitrate
  — Hydralazine
  — Nitroprusside
  — Prazosin
- Dopamine agonist
  — Dopamine
- Analgesics
  — Morphine sulfate
- Anticoagulants
  — Warfarin
  — Aspirin

Nursing Management

- Activity
  — Regular exercise strongly encouraged—improves function of skeletal muscle more than changes in myocardial function

- Diet
  — Limit sodium intake
  — Fluid restriction only if Na^+ <132 mg/dL
  — Avoid excessive fluids
  — Avoid alcohol—depresses myocardial contractility
  — If CAD, low cholesterol, low fat, low Na^+

Inflammatory Heart Disease

- Endocarditis
  — S/S: fever, murmur, heart failure symptoms
  — Infective endocarditis can lead to damaged heart valves
  — Administer antibiotics for 4-6 weeks
  — Teach about anticoagulant therapy
- Pericarditis
  — S/S: Pain—hurts more with deep breath, pericardial friction rub
  — Monitor for ST-segment elevation
  — Monitor hemodynamic status

Valvular Heart Disease

- Valves may be unable to:
  — Fully open (stenosis)
  — Fully close (insufficiency or regurgitation)
- Causes
  — Rheumatic fever
  — Congenital heart disease
  — Syphilis
  — Endocarditis
  — Hypertension

Mitral Valve Stenosis

- Early period—may have no symptoms
- Later—excessive fatigue, dyspnea on exertion, orthopnea, dry cough, hemoptysis, or pulmonary edema
- Rumbling apical diastolic murmur and atrial fibrillation are common

Nursing Plans and Interventions

- See section on congestive heart failure
- Monitor of a-fib with thrombus formation
- Prophylactic antibiotic therapy before any invasive procedures (dental, surgical, childbirth)
- May require surgical repair or valve replacement
- Teaching concerning need for lifelong anticoagulant therapy if valve replacement done

The nurse receives report on four clients on the cardiac unit. Which client should the nurse assess first? The client who has
A. Thrombophlebitis and a positive Homans' sign
B. Left-sided heart failure and an S_3 gallop
C. Pericarditis and inspiratory chest pain
D. Halo vision after digitalization

1. Is the item written in a positive or a negative style?

2. Find the key words in the question.

3. Rephrase the question in your own words.

4. Rule out options:
   -
   -
   -

GASTROINTESTINAL SYSTEM

The nurse is ordering afternoon snacks for several clients. Which client will benefit from a milkshake with whole milk and added protein powder? The client who has

A. Cirrhosis
B. Paralytic ileus
C. Cholelithiasis
D. Dumping syndrome

Gastroesophageal Reflux Disease (GERD)

- Not a disease but a syndrome
- Any clinically significant symptomatic condition secondary to reflux of gastric contents into the lower esophagus
- Most common upper GI problem seen in adults

Etiology and Pathophysiology

There is no one single cause of GERD.
- Predisposing conditions
  — Hiatal hernia
  — Incompetent lower esophageal sphincter (LES)
  — Decreased esophageal clearance (ability to clear liquids or food from the esophagus into the stomach) resulting from impaired esophageal motility
  — Decreased gastric emptying

Nursing Assessment

- Heartburn after eating
- Fullness and discomfort after eating
- Ask client what foods seem to aggravate symptoms
- Positive diagnosis from barium swallow or fluoroscopy (hiatal hernia)

Nursing Plans and Interventions

- Encourage small frequent meals
- Sit up while eating and remain upright for 1 hour after eating
- Stop eating 3 hours before bedtime
- Elevate head of bed 4-6 inches

Medications

- Increase LES pressure
  — Cholinergic
    • Bethanechol (Urecholine)
- Promotility
  — Prokinetic
    • Metoclopramide (Reglan)
- Acid neutralizing
  — Antacids
    • Gelusil, Maalox, Mylanta
- Antisecretory
  — H_2-receptor blockers
    • Cimetidine (Tagamet)

1. Is the item written in a positive or a negative style?

2. Find the key words in the question.

3. Rephrase the question in your own words.

4. Rule out options:
   ■
   ■
   ■

- Famotidine (Pepcid)
- Nizatidine (Axid)
- Ranitidine (Zantac)
— Proton pump inhibitors (PPIs)
- Esomeprazole (Nexium)
- Lansoprazole (Prevacid)
- Omeprazole (Prilosec)
- Pantoprazole (Protonix)
- Rabeprazole (Aciphex)
- Cytoprotective
— Alginic acid-antacid
- Gaviscon
— Acid protective
- Sucralfate (Carafate)

Peptic Ulcer Disease

- Significant gastric ulcers are caused by *Helicobacter pylori* bacteria.
- Risk factors include:
— Drugs: NSAIDs, corticosteroids
— Alcohol
— Cigarette smoking
— Trauma

Nursing Assessment

- Left epigastric pain, may radiate to back
- Epigastric pain relieved with food
- Diagnosed with
— Barium swallow
— Upper endoscopy

Nursing Diagnoses

- Acute pain
- Imbalanced nutrition: less than body requirements

Nursing Plans and Interventions

- Onset of symptoms?
- What relieves symptoms?
- Monitor stools for color, consistency, occult blood
- Administer antacids and antibiotics as ordered
- Avoid caffeine
- Small frequent meals are best

Anti-ulcer Drugs

- Antisecretory
— H_2-receptor blockers
- Cimetidine (Tagamet)
- Famotidine (Pepcid)
- Nizatidine (Axid)
- Ranitidine (Zantac)
— Proton pump inhibitors
- Esomeprazole (Nexium)
- Lansoprazole (Prevacid)
- Omeprazole (Prilosec)
- Pantoprazole (Protonix)
- Rabeprazole (Aciphex)

- Anticholinergics
  — Antisecretory and cytoprotective
    - Misoprostol (Cytotec)
  — Cytoprotective
    - Sucralfate (Carafate)
    - Bismuth subsalicylate (Pepto-Bismol)
  — Neutralizing
    - Antacids
  — Antibiotics for *H. pylori*
    - Amoxicillin
    - Metronidazole (Flagyl)
    - Tetracycline
    - Clarithromycin (Biaxin)
- Others
  — Tricyclic antidepressants
    - Imipramine (Tofranil)
    - Doxepin (Sinequan)

Complications

- Uncontrolled bleeding
  — Prepare for immediate surgery
- Dumping syndrome—postop complication
  — Occurs 5 to 30 minutes after eating
  — Vertigo, syncope, tachycardia
  — Small frequent meals
  — High-fat, high-protein, low-CHO diet
  — Avoid liquids with meals

Client Teaching

- Avoid medications such as:
  — Salicylates
  — NSAIDs
- Inform healthcare personnel of history of peptic ulcer disease
- Symptoms of GI bleeding:
  — Dark tarry stools
  — Coffee ground emesis
  — Bright red rectal bleeding

Crohn's Disease

- Affects both small and large intestine
- Right lower quadrant abdominal pain
- Nausea and vomiting
- 3 to 4 stools per day
- Barium enema shows narrowing with areas of strictures separated by segments of normal bowels

Ulcerative Colitis

- Occurs in large bowel and rectum
- Symptoms
  — Diarrhea
  — Abdominal pain
  — Liquid stools, 10 to 20/day
  — Anemia
- Interventions
  — Low-residue, low-fat, high-protein, high-calorie diet
  — No dairy products
  — Tepid fluids
  — Daily calorie count
  — Monitor I & O

HESI Hint

- Opiates tend to depress gastric motility.
- Distended intestinal wall and decreased muscle tone can lead to intestinal perforation.

Potential NCLEX-RN Question Topics

- Expect dietary questions related to foods appropriate for clients with GI disorders
- Client teaching related to lifestyle changes and medications
- Symptoms of GI bleeding

Diverticular Diseases
- Left lower quadrant pain
- S/S of intestinal obstruction
  — Abdominal distention
  — Constipation/diarrhea
- + Barium enema
- Colonoscopy

Nursing Interventions
- High-fiber diet unless inflammation is present
- If inflammation present
  — NPO
  — Then low residue, bland diet
  — Bulk-forming laxatives
  — Avoid heavy lifting, tight clothing, and straining

Intestinal Obstruction
- Mechanical causes
  — Adhesions most common
  — Strangulated hernia
  — Tumors
- Neurogenic causes
  — Paralytic ileus
  — Spinal cord lesion
- Vascular cause
  — Mesenteric artery occlusion

Nursing Assessment
- Sudden abdominal pain
- History of obstruction
- High-pitched bowel sounds with early mechanical obstruction
- Bowel sounds diminished or absent with neurogenic or late mechanical obstruction

Nursing Interventions
- NPO
- IV fluids
- Nasogastric tube to intermittent suction

Colorectal Cancer
- The third most common form of cancer and the second leading cause of cancer-related deaths in the United States
- Adenocarcinoma most common
- Common metastasis to the liver
- Symptoms
  — Rectal bleeding
  — Change in bowel habits
  — Abdominal pain, weight loss, N/V
  — Ribbon-like stool
  — Sensation of incomplete evacuation

Diagnostic Testing

- History and physical examination
- Digital rectal examination
- Testing of stool for occult blood
- Barium enema
- Sigmoidoscopy
- Colonoscopy
- CBC
- Liver function tests
- CT scan of abdomen
- MRI
- Ultrasound
- Carcinoembryonic antigen (CEA) test

Treatment Modalities

- Chemotherapy
- Biological and targeted therapy
- Epidermal growth factor receptor
- Vascular endothelial growth factor
- Radiation therapy
  — Adjunctive or palliative
- Surgical intervention
  — Bowel resection
  — Temporary colostomy
  — Permanent colostomy

Postoperative Care Issues

- Stoma care
  — Loop
  — Double-barrel
  — End stoma
- Incision care
  — Abdominal
  — Perineal
- Packing and drains
  — HemoVac
  — Jackson-Pratt

Stoma Care

- Assessment
  — The stoma should be pink.
  — There is mild to moderate swelling of the stoma the first 2 to 3 weeks after surgery.
- The pouching system
  — Skin barrier
  — Bag or pouch
  — Adhesive
- Help clients cope with the stoma
  — Provide information
  — Teach practical stoma care techniques
  — Help clients address issues surrounding social interactions
    • Employment
    • Body image
    • Sexuality

HESI Hint
Colostomy irrigation:

- Clean skin and stoma with water
- Use cone to dilate stoma
- Use 300 to 500 mL warm water
- Takes 25 to 40 minutes for fluid to return
- Cold water will cause cramping
- Hot water can damage intestinal mucosa

The nurse is caring for a client who is 24 hours post procedure for a hemicolectomy with a temporary colostomy placement. The assessment finds that the client's stoma is dry and dark red. What action should the nurse implement based on this finding?

A. Notify the healthcare provider of the finding
B. Document the finding in the client record
C. Replace the pouch system over the stoma
D. Place petrolatum gauze dressing on stoma

1. Is the item written in a positive or a negative style?

2. Find the key words in the question.

3. Rephrase the question in your own words.

4. Rule out options:
   ▪
   ▪
   ▪

Cirrhosis

- Degeneration of the liver tissue
- A chronic progressive disease

Nursing Assessment

- Early sign: RUQ pain
- History of
  — ETOH abuse
  — Street drug abuse
- Jaundice
- Fruity or musty breath
- Asterixis
- Palmar erythema
- Ascites
- Weight loss

Esophageal Varices

Esophageal varices may rupture.

Treatment

- Esophagogastric balloon
- Blakemore-Sengstaken tube
- Vitamin K
- Blood products
- Coagulation factors

Nursing Interventions

- Monitor for bleeding
  — Avoid injections
  — Maintain pressure for 5 minutes after venipunctures
- Provide skin care
  — Avoid soap
  — Apply lotions
- Monitor fluid and electrolytes
  — Accurate I & O
  — Weigh daily
  — Restrict fluids (1500 mL/day)
  — Abdominal girth

Dietary Teaching

- Protein may need to be restricted
- Low sodium
- Low potassium
- Low fat
- High carbohydrate
- May need to take lactulose (Cephulac) as ammonia detoxicant/stimulant laxative

HESI Hint

- The liver loses its ability to detoxify mercaptan.
- Chalky or clay-colored stool is a result of absence of bilirubin in stool.

Hepatitis

Nursing Assessment

- Fatigue, weakness
- Anorexia, nausea
- Jaundice
- Dark urine
- Joint pain, muscle aches

Nursing Diagnosis

- Alteration in nutrition: Less than body requirements related to decreased liver function
- Acute pain related to pruritus
- Potential for injury related to bleeding tendencies

Pancreatitis

- Acute = Autodigestion of the pancreas
  — Alcohol ingestion and biliary tract disease are major causes.
- Chronic = Progressive, destructive disease
  — Long-term alcohol use is major factor in disease.

Acute Pancreatitis Assessment

- Mid-epigastric pain radiating to back
  — Aggravated by eating, especially fatty meals
  — Aggravated by alcohol intake
- Abdominal guarding—rigid boardlike abdomen
- Grey-Turner's sign—bluish discoloration of flank
- Cullen's sign—bluish discoloration of periumbilical area
- Elevated amylase, lipase, and glucose

Chronic Pancreatitis Assessment

- Steatorrhea
- Diarrhea
- Jaundice
- Ascites
- Weight loss

Nursing Plans and Interventions

- Acute management
  — NPO
  — NG tube to suction
  — Demerol or morphine for pain management
  — Sitting up or leaning forward may reduce pain
  — Monitor blood sugar
  — Teach foods and fluids to avoid
- Chronic management
  — Pain management
    • Demerol
    • Morphine
  — Pancreatic enzymes
    • Creon
    • Viokase
      Mix powdered forms with fruit juice or apple-sauce: avoid mixing with proteins
  — Teach foods and fluids to avoid

HESI Hints

- Remember to make environment conducive for eating
  — No strong odors
  — Have client sit up for meals
  — Provide small frequent meals
- Liver tissue is destroyed by hepatitis
  — Rest and adequate nutrition are essential for regeneration of liver tissue!
- Be able to differentiate between the three most common types of hepatitis (A, B, C)
  — Sources of infection
  — Routes of transmission
  — Incubation period and onset
  — Vaccines available

A client who has an obstruction of the common bile duct caused by cholelithiasis passes clay-colored stools containing streaks of fat. What action should the nurse implement?
A. Auscultate for diminished bowel sounds
B. Send a stool specimen to the lab
C. Document the assessment in the chart
D. Notify the healthcare provider

1. Is the item written in a positive or a negative style?

2. Find the key words in the question.

3. Rephrase the question in your own words.

4. Rule out options:
   ■
   ■
   ■

Cholecystitis and Cholelithiasis

■ Cholecystitis: acute inflammation of the gallbladder
■ Cholelithiasis: formation or presence of gallstones

Nursing Assessment

■ Pain
■ Fever
■ Elevated WBCs
■ Abdominal tenderness
■ Jaundice

Nursing Plans and Interventions

■ Analgesics for pain
■ NPO
■ NG to suction
■ IV antibiotics
■ Low-fat diet
   — Avoid fried, spicy, and fatty foods

Treatment

■ Cholecystitis
   — IV hydration
   — Administer antibiotics
   — Pain management
■ Cholelithiasis
   — Nonsurgical removal
      ● Endoscopic retrograde cholangiopancreatography (ERCP)
      ● Lithotripsy
   — Surgical approach
      ● Cholecystectomy, laparoscopic or open

A client is admitted with gastric ulcer disease and GI bleeding. Which risk factor should the nurse identify in the client's history?
A. Eats heavily seasoned foods
B. Uses NSAIDs daily
C. Consumes alcohol every day
D. Follows an acid-ash diet

1. Is the item written in a positive or a negative style?

2. Find the key words in the question.

3. Rephrase the question in your own words.

4. Rule out options:
   ■
   ■
   ■

53

Which client should the nurse assess first? A client who has

A. Hyperthyroidism exhibiting exophthalmos
B. Diabetes type 1 with an inflamed foot ulcer
C. Cushing's syndrome exhibiting moon faces
D. Addison's disease with tremors and diaphoresis

Thyroid Gland Feedback Loop

Hypothalamus

$\Downarrow$

TRH (+)

Anterior Pituitary

T_3 & T_4 (−)   TSH (+)

Thyroid Gland

Hyperthyroidism
Nursing Assessment

- Enlarged thyroid gland
- Exophthalmos
- Weight loss
- T_3 elevated
- T_4 elevated
- Diarrhea
- Tachycardia
- Bruit over thyroid

Nursing Diagnoses

- Knowledge deficit
- Imbalanced nutrition: less than body requirements

Nursing Plans and Interventions

- Diet: high protein, high calorie, low caffeine, low fiber
- Treatment may trigger hypothyroidism, may need hormone replacement
- Propylthiouracil (PTU) therapy to block the synthesis of T_3 and T_4
- Iodine (^{131}I) therapy to destroy thyroid cells

Surgical Management

- Thyroidectomy
- Check behind neck for drainage
- Support neck when moving client
- Assess for laryngeal edema
- Have trach set, oxygen, and suction equipment at bedside
- Have calcium gluconate at bedside

1. **Is the item written in a positive or a negative style?**

2. **Find the key words in the question.**

3. **Rephrase the question in your own words.**

4. **Rule out options:**
   -
   -
   -

Which adaptation of the environment is most important for the nurse to include in the plan of care for a client with myxedema?
A. Reduce environmental stimuli
B. Prevent direct sunlight entering the room
C. Maintain a warm room temperature
D. Minimize exposure to visitors

Hypothyroidism

- Fatigue
- Bradycardia
- Weight gain
- Constipation
- Periorbital edema
- Cold intolerance
- Low T_3 (<70)
- Low T_4 (<5)

Nursing Plans and Interventions

- Myxedema coma—an acute exacerbation of hypothyroidism—maintain airway!
- Teach medication regimen
- Monitor for side effects of medications
- Monitor bowel program for S/S of constipation

Thyroid Preparations

- Levothyroxine (Synthroid)
  — Monitor heart rate
  — Hold for pulse > 100 beats/min
- Liothyronine (Cytomel)
- Increase metabolic rate
  — Act as synthetic T_4
  — Check hormone levels regularly
  — Avoid food containing iodine
- Levothyroxine (T_4) + liothyronine (T_3) (Liotrix)
  — Fast onset

A client who is diagnosed with Addison's crisis is admitted, and the nurse places a peripheral saline lock. Which prescription should the nurse administer?
A. Calcium
B. Glucose
C. Potassium
D. Iodine

---

1. Is the item written in a positive or a negative style?

2. Find the key words in the question.

3. Rephrase the question in your own words.

4. Rule out options:
   - ■
   - ■
   - ■

1. Is the item written in a positive or a negative style?

2. Find the key words in the question.

3. Rephrase the question in your own words.

4. Rule out options:
   - ■
   - ■
   - ■

Addison's Disease

- Etiology
  - Sudden withdrawl from corticosteroids
  - Hypofunction of adrenal cortex
  - Lack of pituitary ACTH
- Signs and symptoms include
  - Weight loss
  - N/V
  - Hypovolemia
  - Hypoglycemia
  - Hyponatremia
  - Hyperkalemia
  - Loss of body hair
  - Postural hypotension
  - Hyperpigmentation

Nursing Plans and Interventions

- Frequent vital signs
- Weigh daily
- Monitor serum electrolytes
- Diet: high sodium, low potassium, high carbohydrates
- Encourage at least 3 L of fluid per day

Cushing's Syndrome

Excess adrenal corticoid activity caused by adrenal, pituitary, or hypothalamus tumors

Nursing Assessment

- Moon face and edema of lower extremities
- Flat affect
- Obesity
- Abdominal striae
- Buffalo hump (fat deposits)
- Muscle atrophy, weakness
- Dry pale thinning of skin
- Hypertension
- Osteoporosis
- Immunosuppressed
- Hypovolemic
- Hirsutism
- Lab results
  - Hyperglycemia
  - Hypercalcemia
  - Hypernatremia
  - Hypokalemia
  - Increased plasma cortisol levels

Nursing Diagnoses

- Risk for fluid volume excess related to retention of fluids and sodium secondary to increased cortisol levels
- Risk for infection related to poor wound healing and thin skin

HESI Hint

- Addison's crisis is a medical emergency
- Vascular collapse
  - Hypotension
  - Tachycardia
  - Hypoglycemia
- Need rapid IV infusion
- Give IV glucose
- Glucocorticoids: Solu-Cortef

Nursing Plans and Interventions

- Monitor for S/S of infection
- Fever
- Skin lesions
- Elevated WBCs
- Diet:
  — Low sodium
  — Low carbohydrate

A male client who has type 1 diabetes returns to the clinic for follow-up after dietary counseling. The client states that he has been managing his diabetes very closely. Which lab result indicates the client is maintaining tight control of the disease?
A. FBS changes from 135 to 110 mg/dL.
B. SMBG at HS changes from 45 to 90.
C. Glycosylated Hgb changes from 9% to 6%.
D. Urine ketones change from 0 to 3.

Diabetes Mellitus

Nursing assessment

- Integument—skin breakdown
- Eyes—retinal problems, cataracts
- Kidneys—edema, urinary retention
- Periphery—cool skin, ulcerations on extremities, thick nails
- Cardiopulmonary—angina, dyspnea

Type 1 (IDDM)

- Usually occurs in those younger than 30 years old
- Polydipsia
- Polyphagia
- Polyuria
- Ketosis
- Insulin required to manage
- Easily becomes hyperglycemic
- Serum glucose >350 mg/dL
- Venous pH 6.8-7.2
- Low serum bicarbonate
- Large amounts of ketones in the urine

Type 2 (NIDDM)

- Occurs in persons of school age to older, but great increase being seen in children
- Obesity
- Manage with oral hypoglycemic agents and diet
- Ketoacidosis rare
- Can develop nonketotic hyperosmolar hyperglycemia
- Watch for dehydration
- Mental status changes

Nursing Plans and Interventions

- Teach injection techniques
- Refrigerate unopened insulin

1. Is the item written in a positive or a negative style?

2. Find the key words in the question.

3. Rephrase the question in your own words.

4. Rule out options:
   - ■
   - ■
   - ■

HESI Hints

- Review S/S of hypoglycemia and hyperglycemia
- Review clinical characteristics and treatment protocols for types of diabetes
- Be familiar with glycosylated hemoglobin test (Hgb A_{1C}), which indicates glucose control over previous 120 days

- Diet
  — 55%-60% carbohydrate
  — 12%-15% protein
  — 30% fat
- Exercise regimen
- Establish a regular routine
- Plan meals and snacks around exercise routine
- May need snack before or during exercise
- Monitor for S/S of hypoglycemia
- Foot care
  — Check daily
  — Report signs of injury
- Manage sick days
  — Keep taking insulin
  — Check blood sugar more frequently
  — Watch for S/S of hyperglycemia

Oral Hypoglycemics

- Sulfonylureas
  — Glimepiride (Amaryl)
  — Glipizide (Glucotrol)
  — Glyburide (Micronase)
- Biguanide
  — Metformin (Glucophage)
- Alpha-glucosidase inhibitors
  — Acarbose (Precose)
  — Miglitol (Glyset)
- Thiazolidinediones
  — Pioglitazone (Actos)
  — Rosiglitazone (Avandia)
- Meglitinides
  — Repaglinide (Prandin)
- Combinations
  — Glyburide/metformin (Glucovance)

Types/Actions of Insulin

- Rapid acting
  — Lispro, NovoLog
    - Onset 5 to 15 min
    - Peak 45 to 90 min
    - Give within 15 min of meals
    - May NOT be given IV
- Short acting
  — Regular
    - Onset 30 to 60 min
    - Peak 2 to 3 hr
    - Give 30 min before meals
    - May be given IV
- Intermediate acting
  — NPH
    - Onset 1 to 2 hr
    - Peak 6 to 12 hr
    - May NOT be given IV
- Long acting
  — Lantus glargine
    - Onset 1 to 5 hr
    - No real peak
    - Once daily at bedtime
    - May NOT be given IV

- Premixes
  — Humalog 75/25
  — Human 70/30
  — Humalog 70/30

MUSCULOSKELETAL SYSTEM

Which action by the unlicensed assistive personnel (UAP) requires immediate follow-up by the nurse?

A. Positions a client who is 12 hours post–above-knee amputation (AKA) with the residual limb elevated on a pillow

B. Assists a client with ambulation while the client uses a cane on the unaffected side

C. Accompanies a client who has lupus erythematosus to sit outside in the sun during a break

D. Helps a client with rheumatoid arthritis to the bathroom after the client receives Celebrex

1. **Is the item written in a positive or a negative style?**

2. **Find the key words in the question.**

3. **Rephrase the question in your own words.**

4. **Rule out options:**
   - ■
   - ■
   - ■

Rheumatoid Arthritis

- Chronic, systemic, progressive deterioration of the connective tissue
- Etiology: unknown, believed to be autoimmune

Nursing Assessment

- Young to middle age
- More females than males
- Systemic with exacerbating and remissions
- Small joints first, then spreads
- Stiffness (may decrease with use)
- Decreased range of motion
- Joint pain
- Elevated erythrocyte sedimentation rate (ESR)
- Positive rheumatoid factor (RF) in 80% of clients
- Narrowed joint space

Nursing Plans and Interventions
Drug therapy

- High-dose ASA or NSAIDs
- Systemic corticosteroids
- Disease-modifying antirheumatic drugs (DMARDs)
  — Methotrexate (Rheumatrex)
  — Sulfasalazine (Azulfidine)
  — Hydroxychloroquine (Plaquenil)
  — Leflunomide (Arava)
- Heat and cold applications
- Weight management
- Rest and joint protection
- Use assistive devices
- Shower chair
- Canes, walkers
- Straight back chairs, elevated seats

Lupus Erythematosus

- Two classifications of lupus erythematosus
  — Discoid lupus erythematosus (DLE): Affects skin only
  — Systemic lupus erythematosus (SLE): More prevalent than DLE

- Major trigger factors
  — Sunlight
  — Infectious agents
  — Stress
  — Drugs
  — Pregnancy

Nursing Assessment
- DLE: scaly rash, butterfly rash over bridge of nose
- SLE: joint pain, fever, nephritis, pericarditis (see figure)
- Photosensitivity

Nursing Diagnoses
- Impaired skin integrity related to decreased mobility and circulation
- Pain related to joint swelling

Nursing Plans and Interventions
- Teaching
  — Drugs
  — Pain management
  — Disease process
  — Conservation of energy
  — Avoid prolonged exposure to ultraviolet rays
  — Avoid/reduce stress
  — Use mild soaps, creams for skin care
  — Use of steroids for joint inflammation
- Therapeutic exercise and heat therapy
- Marital and pregnancy counseling

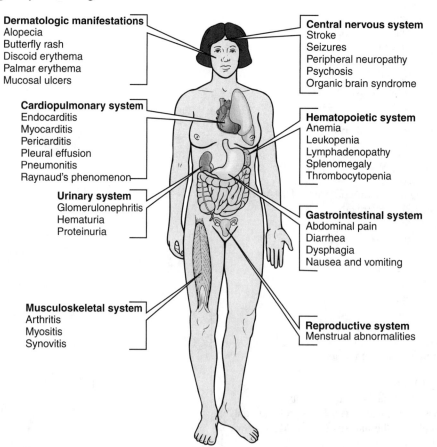

Dermatologic manifestations
Alopecia
Butterfly rash
Discoid erythema
Palmar erythema
Mucosal ulcers

Central nervous system
Stroke
Seizures
Peripheral neuropathy
Psychosis
Organic brain syndrome

Cardiopulmonary system
Endocarditis
Myocarditis
Pericarditis
Pleural effusion
Pneumonitis
Raynaud's phenomenon

Hematopoietic system
Anemia
Leukopenia
Lymphadenopathy
Splenomegaly
Thrombocytopenia

Urinary system
Glomerulonephritis
Hematuria
Proteinuria

Gastrointestinal system
Abdominal pain
Diarrhea
Dysphagia
Nausea and vomiting

Musculoskeletal system
Arthritis
Myositis
Synovitis

Reproductive system
Menstrual abnormalities

Degenerative Joint Disease (Osteoarthritis)

- Joint pain increases with activity
- Morning stiffness
- Crepitus
- Limited movement
- Joint enlargements

Nursing Plans and Interventions

- Follow weight reduction diet
- Excessive use of involved joint may accelerate degeneration
- Use proper body mechanics
- Keep joints in functional position
- Hot and cold applications for pain and stiffness
- NSAIDs, opioid analgesics, and intra-articular corticosteroids

A postmenopausal woman who has a BMI of 18 is at the clinic for her annual well-woman's exam. Which teaching plan topic should the nurse prepare for this high-risk client?

A. Osteoporosis
B. Obesity
C. Anorexia
D. Breast cancer

Osteoporosis
Risk Factors

- Small postmenopausal females
- Diet low in calcium
- Excessive alcohol, tobacco, and caffeine
- Inactive lifestyle
- Low testosterone level in men

Nursing Assessment

- Dowager's hump
- Kyphosis of the dorsal spine
- Loss of height
- Pathological fractures
- Compression fracture of spine can occur

Nursing Plans and Interventions

- Keep bed in low position
- Provide adequate lighting
- Avoid using throw rugs
- Provide assistance with ambulation
- Follow regular exercise program
- Diet high in vitamin D, protein, and calcium

Drug Therapy

- Bisphosphonates
  — Alendronate (Fosamax)
  — Clodronate (Bonefos)
  — Etidronate (Didronel)

1. **Is the item written in a positive or a negative style?**

2. **Find the key words in the question.**

3. **Rephrase the question in your own words.**

4. **Rule out options:**
   -
   -
   -

NCLEX QUESTION FOCUS

- Safety precautions for clients with degenerative joint disease (DJD) or osteoporosis
- Remember proper technique for using assistive devices, household safety measures!

— Ibandronate (Boniva)
— Pamidronate (Aredia)
— Risedronate (Actonel)
— Tiludronate (Skelid)
- Selective estrogen receptor modulator
— Raloxifene (Evista)
— Teriparatide (Forteo)

Fractures
Signs and Symptoms
- Pain, swelling, deformity of the extremity
- Discoloration, loss of functional ability
- Fracture evident on x-ray

Nursing Plans and Interventions
- Instruct on proper use of assistive devices
— Crutches, cane, or walker
- Assess for the 5 Ps of neurovascular functioning
— Pain, paresthesia, pulse, pallor, and paralysis
- Assess neurovascular area distal to injury
— Skin color, temperature, sensation, capillary refill, mobility, pain, and pulses
- Intervention
— Closed reduction
— Open reduction
- Post reduction
— Cast
— Traction
— External fixation
— Splints
— Orthoses (braces)

Joint Replacement
- Following surgery
— Check circulation, sensation, and movement of extremity distal to replacement area
— Keep body in proper alignment
— Encourage fluid intake
— Use of bedpan, commode chair
— Coordinate rehabilitation process
- Discharge home
— Safety
— Accessibility
- Drugs
— Anticoagulants
— Analgesics
— Parenteral antibiotics

Amputation
- Postop care will include:
— Monitoring surgical dressing for drainage
— Proper body alignment
— Elevate residual limb (stump) first 24 hr
— Do NOT elevate after 48 hr
— Provide passive range of motion (ROM) and encourage prone position periodically to decrease risk of contracture
— Proper stump bandaging to prepare for prosthesis
— Coordination of care with OT and PT

NCLEX Question Focus
- Complications
— Infection
— Embolus
— Anemia
— Skin integrity
— Urinary calculi

Amputation Drugs

- Analgesics
  — Phantom pain is REAL
- Antibiotics

The nurse is assessing a client who is scheduled for surgical fixation of a compound fracture of the right ulna. Which finding should the nurse report to the healthcare provider?

A. Ecchymosis around the fracture site
B. Crepitus at the fracture site
C. Paresthesia distal to the fracture site
D. Diminished range of motion of the right arm

NEUROSENSORY AND NEUROLOGICAL SYSTEMS

The nurse observes an elderly client with glaucoma administer eye drops by tilting his head back, instilling each drop close to the inner canthus, and keeping his eye closed for 15 seconds. What action should the nurse implement first?

A. Ask the client if another family member is available to administer the drops
B. Review the correct steps of the procedure with the client
C. Administer the eye drops correctly in the other eye to demonstrate the technique
D. Discuss the importance of correct eye drop administration for persons with glaucoma

Glaucoma

- Primary open-angle glaucoma
  — Drainage channels become clogged
  — Decrease flow trabecular meshwork
- Primary closure-angle glaucoma
  — Bulging lens disrupts flow
- The silent thief of vision
- Normally painless
- Loss of peripheral vision
- May see halos around lights
- Diagnosed with eye exam
  — Tonometer to measure intraocular pressure
  — Electronic tonometer to detect aqueous humor drainage

Nursing Plans and Interventions

- Key to treatment is:
  — ↓ Intraocular pressure
    • ↓ Aqueous humor production
    • ↑ Drainage of aqueous humor
  — Teach client and family proper eye drop instillation
  — Teach client how to avoid activities that can increase intraocular pressure

1. Is the item written in a positive or a negative style?

2. Find the key words in the question.

3. Rephrase the question in your own words.

4. Rule out options:
   -
   -
   -

1. Is the item written in a positive or a negative style?

2. Find the key words in the question.

3. Rephrase the question in your own words.

4. Rule out options:
   -
   -
   -

63

Treatment

Collaborative therapy

- Ambulatory/home care for open-angle glaucoma
  — Drug therapy
    - β-Adrenergic blockers
    - α-Adrenergic agonists
    - Cholinergic agents (miotics)
    - Carbonic anhydrase inhibitors
  — Surgical therapy
    - Argon laser trabeculoplasty (ALT)
    - Trabeculectomy with or without filtering implant
- Acute care for closure-angle glaucoma
  — Topical cholinergic agent
  — Hyperosmotic agent
  — Laser peripheral iridotomy
  — Surgical iridectomy

Drug therapy

- β-Adrenergic blockers
  — Betaxolol (Betoptic)
  — Levobunolol (Betagan)
  — Metipranolol (OptiPranolol)
  — Timolol maleate (Timoptic, Istalol)
- α-Adrenergic agonists
  — Dipivefrin (Propine)
  — Epinephrine (Epifrin, Eppy, Gaucon, Epitrate, Epinal, Eppy/N)
  — Apraclonidine (Lopidine)
  — Brimonidine (Alphagan)
  — Latanoprost (Xalatan)
- Cholinergic agents (Miotics)
  — Carbachol (Isopto Carbachol)
  — Pilocarpine (Akarpine; IsoptoCarpine, Pilocar, Pilopine, Piloptic, Pilostat)
- Carbonic anhydrase inhibitors
  — Systemic
    - Acetazolamide (Diamox)
    - Dichlorphenamide (Daranide)
    - Methazolamide (Neptazane)
  — Topical
    - Brinzolamide (Azopt)
    - Dorzolamide (Trusopt)
- Combination therapy
  — Timolol maleate and dorzolamide (Cosopt)
- Hyperosmolar agents
  — Glycerin liquid (Ophthalgan, Osmoglyn Oral)
  — Isosorbide solution (Ismotic)
  — Mannitol solution (Osmitrol)

Cataracts

- Clouding or opacity of the lens
- Early signs
  — Blurred vision
  — Decreased color perception
- Late signs
  — Double vision
  — Clouded pupil

Nursing Plans and Interventions for Cataract Removal

■ Preop
  — Assess medications being taken
  — Anticoagulants should be stopped prior to surgery
  — Teach how to instill eye drops
■ Postop
  — Eye shield should be worn during sleeping hours
  — Avoid lifting >15 pounds
  — Avoid lying on operative side
  — Report signs of increased intraocular pressure
    • Acute pain

Eye Trauma/Injury

■ Trauma
  — Determine type of injury
  — Position client in sitting position to decrease intra-ocular pressure
  — Never attempt to remove embedded object
  — Irrigate eye if a chemical injury has occurred
■ Detached retina
  — Described as curtain falling over visual field
  — Painless
  — May have black spots or floaters (indicates bleeding has occurred with detachment)
  — Surgical repair of retina
  — Keep eye patch over affected area

Hearing Loss

■ Conductive hearing loss
  — Sounds do not travel to the inner ear
  — May benefit from hearing aid
■ Sensorineural hearing loss
  — Sound distorted from defect in inner ear

Sensorineural Loss

■ Common causes
  — Infections
  — Ototoxic drugs
■ Gentamicin
■ Vancomycin
■ Lasix
  — Trauma
  — Aging process
■ Assessment
  — Inability to hear whisper from 1 to 2 feet away
  — Shouting in conversations
  — Turning head to favor one ear
  — Loud volume on TV

Altered State of Consciousness

■ Glasgow Coma Scale
  — Used to assess level of consciousness
  — Maximum score 15, minimum 3
  — A score of 7 or less = coma
  — Score of 3 to 4 = high mortality rate
  — Score of >8 = good prognosis

HESI Hint

■ NCLEX questions will focus on communication and safety with the older adult
  — Speak in low-pitched voice
  — Face client
  — Use appropriate visual aids
  — Don't switch topics
  — Keep external noise to a minimum

Neurological Vital Signs

- Pupil size (with sizing scale)
- Limb movement (with scale)
- Vital signs (blood pressure, temperature, pulse, respirations)

Nursing Plans and Interventions

- Assess for early S/S of changes in level of consciousness (LOC)
  — Decreasing LOC
  — Change in orientation
- Late signs
  — Cushing's triad
    - Widening pulse pressure
    - Slowing heart rate
    - Slowing respirations
  — Change in size, response of pupils—dilate on side of injury initially
  — Elevated temperature

Nursing Assessment and Interventions

- Assess for change in respiratory status
  — Cheyne–Stokes respiration
  — Maintain airway: with decreasing LOC will need mechanical ventilation
- Prevent hypoxia
- Keep Pco_2 at 28 to 30 mm Hg
- Hyperventilate (hyperoxygenate) before suctioning
- Limit suctioning to 15 seconds
  — Keep airway free of secretions
  — Prevent aspiration

Nutritional Care for the Unconscious Client

- Keep NPO
- Administer hyperalimentation or tube feedings as ordered
- Prevent aspiration
- Maintain a calorie count

Which change in the status of a client being treated for increased ICP warrants immediate action by the nurse?
A. Urinary output changes from 20 to 50 mL/hr.
B. Arterial Pco_2 changes from 40 to 30 mm Hg.
C. Glasgow Coma Scale score changes from 5 to 7.
D. Pulse changes from 88 to 68 beats/min.

Head Injury

- Assessment
  — Changes in LOC
  — Signs of increased intracranial pressure (ICP)
  — Changes in VS
  — Headache

HESI Hints

- Understand why it is important to quickly decrease an elevated temperature
- Be aware of nursing actions to ensure safety for immobilized clients
- Remember that while restlessness may indicate a return to consciousness, it may also indicate anoxia, bleeding, or distended bladder
- Do not oversedate, and report restlessness

1. **Is the item written in a positive or a negative style?**

2. **Find the key words in the question.**

3. **Rephrase the question in your own words.**

4. **Rule out options:**
   -
   -
   -

— Vomiting
— Pupillary changes
— Seizure
— Ataxia
— Abnormal posturing (decerebrate or decorticate)

CSF Leakage
- Risk for meningitis with leakage
- May not see usual signs of increased ICP with leakage of CSF
- Drainage may come from nose (rhinorrhea) or ears (otorrhea)

Nursing Diagnoses
- Altered cerebral tissue perfusion related to ↑ ICP
  — To determine altered tissue perfusion, calculate the cerebral perfusion pressure (CPP) from the mean arterial pressure (MAP) and the intracranial pressure (ICP):
    - $MAP - ICP = CPP$
    - Amount of blood flow from systemic circulation required to provide oxygen to the brain
    - Ideally CPP should be >70 mm Hg
- Ineffective breathing pattern related to ischemia

Nursing Interventions
- Neurological assessment every 15 minutes
- Notify MD at FIRST sign of deterioration
- Limit visitors
- Keep room quiet
- Prevent straining
- Keep HOB at 30 to 45 degrees
- Avoid neck flexion/straining
- Monitor I & O

Medical Treatment for Increased Intracranial Pressure
- ICP monitoring
  — Want ICP to be <20 mm Hg
- Hyperosmotic agents
  — 20% mannitol
- Steroids
  — Decadron
  — Solu-Medrol
- Barbiturates
- Prophylactic Dilantin
- Diuretics
  — Alternate with mannitol
- Avoid narcotics!

Spinal Cord Injury
- Injuries are classified by:
  — Extent of injury
  — Level of injury
  — Mechanism of injury
- Injuries are classified as complete or incomplete
  — Transection/partial transection
- Rule of thumb:
  Injury above C8 = quadriplegic
  Injury below C8 = paraplegic

Nursing Assessment

- Start with the ABCs
- Determine quality of respiratory status
- Check neurological status
- Assess vital signs
  — Hypotension and bradycardia occur in injuries above T6

Nursing Diagnoses

- Ineffective breathing pattern related to impaired movement of diaphragm
- Risk for aspiration related to impaired swallowing
- Altered tissue perfusion related to immobility

Nursing Plans and Interventions

- Immobilize and stabilize!
- Keep neck and body in anatomical alignment
- Maintain patent airway
- Cervical injuries will be placed in skeletal traction
- High-dose corticosteroids are used to control edema during first 24 hours
- Spinal shock
  — Flaccid paralysis
  — Complete or near complete loss of reflexes
  — Hypotension
  — Bradycardia
  — Bowel and bladder distention
- Reverse as quickly as possible

Autonomic Dysreflexia

- Medical emergency that occurs in clients with injuries at or above T6
- Exaggerated autonomic reflex response
- Usually triggered by bowel or bladder distention
- S/S: severe headache, ↑ BP, bradycardia, and profuse sweating
- Elevate head of bed (while maintaining correct alignment), relieve bowel or bladder distention

Rehabilitation

- Watch for paralytic ileus
  — Assess bowel sounds
- Kinetic bed to promote blood flow
- Antiembolic stockings
- Protect from skin breakdown
- Bowel and bladder training
  — Keeping bladder empty and urine dilute and acidic to help prevent urinary tract infection, a common cause of death after spinal cord injury

Specific Neurological Disorders
BRAIN TUMOR

- Primary malignant tumors can arise in any area of brain tissue
- Benign tumors can continue to grow and cause problems with ↑ ICP
- Assess for headache, vomiting, seizures, aphasia, abnormal CT, MRI, or PET scan

Nursing Plans and Interventions
- Similar to head injury client
- Major concern is ↑ ICP
- Keep HOB elevated 30 to 40 degrees
- Radiation therapy
- Chemotherapy
- Surgical removal
- Craniotomy
- Postop care
  — Monitor for ↑ ICP
  — CSF leakage
  — Monitor respiratory status closely
  — Monitor for seizure activity

MULTIPLE SCLEROSIS
- Demyelination of the central nervous system (CNS) myelin
- Messages are garbled
- Messages are short-circuited from the brain to the CNS
- Disease is characterized by periods of remissions and exacerbations
- Assessment findings include:
  — Changes in visual field
  — Weaknesses in extremities
  — Numbness
  — Visual or swallowing difficulties
  — Unusual fatigue
  — Gait disturbances

Nursing Diagnoses and Interventions
- Impaired sensory alterations
  — Keep objects labeled
  — Avoid quick changes in room lighting
- Impaired mobility
  — Provide assistive devices
- Impaired swallowing
  — Thickened liquid

Drug Therapy
- Focus on controlling symptoms
- Corticosteroids
  — ACTH, prednisone, methylprednisolone
- Immunomodulators
  — Interferon beta (Betaseron, Avonex, Rebif)
  — Glatiramer acetate (Copaxone)
- Immunosuppressants
  — Mitoxantrone (Novantrone)
- Cholinergics
  — Bethanechol (Urecholine)
  — Neostigmine (Prostigmin)
- Anticholinergics
  — Propantheline (Pro-Banthine)
  — Oxybutynin (Ditropan)
- Muscle relaxants
  — Diazepam (Valium)
  — Baclofen (Lioresal)
  — Dantrolene (Dantrium)
  — Tizanidine (Zanaflex)

- CNS stimulants
  — Pemoline (Cylert)
  — Methylphenidate (Ritalin)
  — Modafinil (Provigil)
- Antiviral/antiparkinsonian drugs
  — Symmetrel (Amantadine)

MYASTHENIA GRAVIS

- A chronic neuromuscular autoimmune disease
- Caused by loss of ACh receptors in the postsynaptic neurons at the neuromuscular junction
- ACh is necessary for muscles to contract
- Causes weakness and abnormal fatigue of voluntary muscles

Nursing Assessment

- Ocular muscle weakness
- Bulbar muscle weakness
- Skeletal muscle weakness

Diagnosis

- Based upon clinical presentation
  — Muscle weakness
- Confirmed by testing response to anticholinesterase drugs
- Tensilon test—2 mg IV

Medications

- Anticholinesterase agents
  — Try to achieve maximum strength and endurance
  — Blocks action of cholinesterase
  — Increase levels of ACh at junctions
  — Common medications
    - Mestinon
    - Prostigmin
  — Start with minimal doses
  — Onset 30 minutes
  — Duration 3 to 4 hours
  — Must take on time!
- Corticosteroids
  — Prednisone
- Immunosuppressive agents
  — Azathioprine (Imuran)
  — Cyclophosphamide (Cytoxan)

Types of Crisis

- Myasthenic
  — MEDICAL EMERGENCY!
  — Caused by undermedication or infection
  — Positive Tensilon test
  — Changes in VS, cyanosis, loss of cough and gag reflex, incontinence
  — May require intubation
- Cholinergic
  — Results from overmedication
  — Toxic levels of anticholinesterase medications
  — Symptoms: abdominal cramps, diarrhea, excessive pulmonary secretions
  — Negative Tensilon test

70

Nursing Diagnoses and Interventions

- Ineffective breathing pattern related to impaired respiratory muscles
  — Coughing and deep breathing exercises
  — Suction equipment at bedside
- Imbalanced nutrition: less than body requirements related to impaired swallowing
  — Sit upright when eating and 1 hour after
  — Keep chin downward when swallowing
- High risk for injury related to sensory perceptual disturbances
  — Plan activities carefully, weakness is greater at the end of the day
- Impaired verbal communication
- Disturbed sensory perception

PARKINSON'S DISEASE

Triad of symptoms

- Rigidity
  — Mask-like face
- Akinesia
  — Difficulty initiating and continuing movement
- Tremors
  — Resting tremors
  — Pill rolling

Drug Therapy

- Dopaminergics
  — Levodopa (L-dopa, dopamine)
    • Blocks breakdown of levodopa to allow more levodopa to cross the blood-brain barrier
    • Avoid foods high in vitamin B_6 and high-protein foods
  — Levodopa-carbidopa (Sinemet, Paracopa [orally dissolving tablet])
    • Allows for less use of levodopa and helps decrease side effects
  — Bromocriptine mesylate (Parlodel)
    • Helps with motor fluctuations
  — Pergolide (Permax)
  — Pramipexole (Mirapex)
  — Ropinirole (Requip)
  — Amantadine (Symmetrel)
  — Apomorphine (Apokyn)
- Anticholinergics: treat tremors
  — Trihexyphenidyl (Artane)
  — Benztropine (Cogentin)
  — Biperiden (Akineton)
- Antihistamine
  — Diphenhydramine (Benadryl)
- Monoamine oxidase inhibitors
  — Selegiline (Eldepryl, Carbex)
  — Rasagiline (Azilect)
- Catechol-O-methyl transferase (COMT) inhibitors
  — Entacapone (Comtan)
  — Tolcapone (Tasmar)

Nursing Plans and Interventions

- SAFETY is always a priority!
- Take medications with meals
- Change positions slowly to decrease postural hypotension
- Thicken liquids
- Soft ground foods
- Encourage activity and exercise

GUILLAIN-BARRE SYNDROME

- Usually occurs after an upper respiratory infection
- Ascending paralysis
- Rapid demyelination of the nerves
- Paralysis of respiratory system may occur quickly
- Prepare to intubate
- Treatment
  - Plasmapheresis over 10 to 15 days
  - IV high-dose immunoglobulin (Sandoglobulin) is effective as plasma exchange and has the advantage of immediate availability and greater safety. Clients receiving high-dose immunoglobulin need to be well hydrated and have adequate renal function.
  - Maintain patent airway
  - Reposition frequently
  - Impaired swallowing—may need TPN
  - Supervise feedings

STROKE (BRAIN ATTACK) OR CEREBROVASCULAR ACCIDENT

- Hemorrhagic—hemorrhage into brain tissue
- Ischemic—clot
  - Thrombolytic
  - Embolic
- Diagnosed by presenting symptoms, CT, MRI, and Doppler flow studies
- Causes paralysis, aphagia (Broca's, Wernicke's, and global aphasia are all common)

Nursing Plans and Interventions

- Assess for S/S of increased ICP
- Assess verbal ability and plan care appropriate to client's ability to communicate
- Assess swallowing—prevent aspiration
- Assess for bowel and bladder control
- Assess functional abilities
  - Mobility
  - Activities of daily living (ADLs)
  - Elimination

Which client is best to assign to a graduate nurse being oriented to the neurological unit?

A. A head-injured client with a Glasgow Coma Scale score of 6

B. A client who develops autonomic dysreflexia following a T6 spinal cord injury

C. A client with multiple sclerosis who needs the first dose of interferon

D. A client suspected of having Guillain-Barré syndrome

HESI Hint

- Review differences in client assessment data bases on whether the disruption was in the left or right hemisphere
  - Language
  - Memory
  - Vision
  - Behavior
  - Hearing

1. **Is the item written in a positive or a negative style?**

2. **Find the key words in the question.**

3. **Rephrase the question in your own words.**

4. **Rule out options:**
   -
   -
   -

Which client should the nurse assess first? A client receiving

A. Oxygen per nasal cannula who is dyspneic with mild exertion and has a hemoglobin of 7 g/dL
B. IV aminoglycosides per CVC who complains of nausea and has a trough level below therapeutic levels
C. Packed RBCs who complains of flank pain and has a BP of 98/52 mm Hg
D. Chemotherapy whose temperature is 98.9° F and has a WBC count of 2500/mm³

1. Is the item written in a positive or a negative style?

2. Find the key words in the question.

3. Rephrase the question in your own words.

4. Rule out options:
   -
   -
   -

Anemia

- Decreased erythrocyte production
- Decreased hemoglobin synthesis
  — Iron deficiency anemia
  — Thalassemias (decreased globin synthesis)
  — Sideroblastic anemia (decreased porphyrin)
- Defective DNA synthesis
  — Cobalamin (vitamin B_{12}) deficiency
  — Folic acid deficiency
- Decreased number of erythrocyte precursors
  — Aplastic anemia
- Anemia of myeloproliferative diseases (e.g., leukemia) and myelodysplasia
- Chronic diseases or disorders
- Chemotherapy
- Blood loss
  — Acute
  — Trauma
- Blood vessel rupture
- Chronic
- Gastritis
- Menstrual flow
- Hemorrhoids
- Increased erythrocyte destruction

Intrinsic Causes

- Abnormal hemoglobin (HbS–sickle cell anemia)
- Enzyme deficiency (G6PD)
- Membrane abnormalities (paroxysmal nocturnal hemoglobinuria, hereditary spherocytosis)

Extrinsic Causes

- Physical trauma (prosthetic heart valves, extracorporeal circulation)
- Antibodies (isoimmune and autoimmune)
- Infectious agents, medications, and toxins

Nursing Assessment

- Pallor
- Fatigue
- Exercise intolerance
- Tachycardia
- Dyspnea
- Assess for risk factors

- Diet low in iron, vitamin B_{12} deficiency, history of bleeding, medications taken
  — Hgb <10, Hct <36, RBC <4

Nursing Plans and Interventions
- Treatment of underlying pathology
- Administer blood products as ordered
- Diet should be high in iron-rich foods, folic acid, vitamin B_{12}, vitamin B_6, amino acids, and vitamin C
- Parenteral iron is given using Z-track technique

Leukemia
Types of leukemia
- Acute myelogenous leukemia (AML)
  — Inability of leukocytes to mature; those that do are abnormal
  — 60-70 years old
- Chronic myelogenous leukemia (CML)
  — Abnormal production of granulocytic cells
  — 20-60 years of age (peak around 45 years)
- Acute lymphocytic leukemia (ALL)
  — Abnormal leukocytes in blood-forming tissue
  — Before 14 years of age and older adults
- Chronic lymphocytic leukemia (CLL)
  — Increased production of leukocytes and lymphocytes within the bone marrow, spleen, and liver
  — 50-70 years of age

Nursing Assessment
- General
  — Fever, generalized lymphadenopathy, lethargy
- Integumentary
  — Pallor or jaundice; petechiae, ecchymoses, purpura, reddish brown to purple cutaneous infiltrates, macules, and papules
- Cardiovascular
  — Tachycardia, systolic murmurs
- Gastrointestinal
  — Gingival bleeding and hyperplasia; oral ulcerations, herpes and *Candida* infections; perirectal irritation and infection; hepatomegaly, splenomegaly
- Neurological
  — Seizures, disorientation, confusion, decreased coordination, cranial nerve palsies, papilledema
- Musculoskeletal
  — Muscle wasting, bone pain, joint pain

Medications for Leukemia
- Alkylating agents
- Antimetabolites
- Corticosteroids
- Nitrosoureas
- Mitotic inhibitors/vinca alkaloids
- Biological/targeted therapy
- Podophyllotoxin
- Retinoid

NCLEX QUESTION FOCUS
- Choosing appropriate foods in the diet to instruct the client about
  — Iron – red meats, whole wheat, spinach
  — Folic acid – green vegetables
  — Vitamin B_{12} – yeast, milk, green leafy vegetables

Nursing Plans and Interventions for Clients with Immunodeficiency and/or Bone Marrow Suppression

- Monitor WBC count
- Report fever or S/S of infection to physician as soon as symptoms are recognized
- Teach infection control measures
- Administer IV antibiotics as ordered:
  — Trough (draw shortly before administration)
  — Peak (30 minutes to 1 hour after administration)

Lymphomas
HODGKIN'S LYMPHOMA
Etiology

— Epstein-Barr virus (EBV), genetic predisposition, and exposure to occupational toxins

Diagnosis

— The main diagnostic feature of Hodgkin's lymphoma is the presence of Reed-Sternberg cells in lymph node biopsy specimens.

Nursing Assessment

— Weight loss
— Fatigue
— Weakness
— Chills, fever, night sweats
— Tachycardia

Nursing Interventions

— Chemotherapy
— Radiation therapy
— Pain management due to tumors
— Pancytopenia
— Fertility
— Secondary malignancies

NON-HODGKIN'S LYMPHOMA
Etiology

— Immunosuppressant medications, age and HIV, Epstein-Barr virus (EBV)
— Affects the beta or T cells

Diagnosis

— Same as for Hodgkin's lymphoma
— MRI, CT scan, and barium enemas

Nursing Assessment
- — Painless lymph node enlargement (lymphadenopathy)
- — Depending on where the disease has spread
- — Same as Hodgkin's lymphoma

Nursing Interventions
- — Chemotherapy (sometimes radiation therapy)
- — Monoclonal antibodies
- — Symptom management (depending on affected system)

Nursing Diagnoses
- — Risk for infection related to immunosuppression
- — Imbalanced nutrition: less than body requirements related to anorexia

Nursing Plans and Interventions
- — Strict aseptic technique
- — Protect client from infection
- — Monitor for S/S of anemia
- — High-nutrient diet
- — Emotional support to client and family
- — Treatment needs to be completed to help ensure survival
- — Highly curable disease when diagnosed early and treatment is completed

A client is receiving vancomycin (Vancocin) IV and has a prescription for peak and trough levels. Before administering the next dose, what action should the nurse implement?
A. Verify the culture and sensitivity results.
B. Review the client's WBC count.
C. Schedule the collection of blood for a peak level.
D. Determine if the trough level has been collected.

Administration of Chemotherapeutic Agents
- Strict guidelines must be followed!
- Normally administered by chemotherapy certified RN
- Pregnant nurses should not administer most of these agents
- Wear gloves when handling drugs
- Types of IV catheters
  - — Hickman
  - — Broviac
  - — Port-a-cath

1. Is the item written in a positive or a negative style?

2. Find the key words in the question.

3. Rephrase the question in your own words.

4. Rule out options:
  - ■
  - ■
  - ■

HESI Hints
- Be familiar with oncology terms
- Be familiar with the "carcinoma" prefixes or pre-words such as "adeno" "osteo"—this will help you identify the tissue of origin.

A client who is receiving chemotherapy has a CBC result showing a hemoglobin of 8.5 g/dL, hematocrit of 32%, and WBC count of 6500 cells/mm3. Which meal choice is best?

A. Grilled chicken, rice, fresh fruit salad, milk
B. Broiled steak, whole wheat rolls, spinach salad, coffee
C. Smoked ham, mashed potatoes, applesauce, iced tea
D. Tuna noodle casserole, garden salad, lemonade

1. Is the item written in a positive or a negative style?

2. Find the key words in the question.

3. Rephrase the question in your own words.

4. Rule out options:
   ▪
   ▪
   ▪

REPRODUCTIVE SYSTEM

A 52-year-old who had an abdominal hysterectomy for a grade III Pap smear is preparing for discharge. Which recommendation should the nurse offer the client about women's health and screening exams?

A. Continue your annual Pap smears, mammogram, clinical breast exam, and continue monthly breast self-exam (BSE).
B. A Pap smear is no longer necessary, but continue annual mammogram and clinical breast exam, plus monthly BSE.
C. Without ovaries, only an annual mammogram and clinical breast exam are necessary.
D. Annual mammograms are not needed if biannual clinical breast exams and weekly BSE are done.

1. Is the item written in a positive or a negative style?

2. Find the key words in the question.

3. Rephrase the question in your own words.

4. Rule out options:
   ▪
   ▪
   ▪

Benign Uterine Tumors
▪ Arise from muscle tissue of the uterus
▪ Signs and symptoms:
   — Menorrhagia
   — Uterine enlargement
   — Dysmenorrhea
   — Anemia secondary to menorrhagia
   — Uterine enlargement
   — Low back pain and pelvic pain
▪ Tend to disappear after menopause
▪ Surgical options:
   — Myomectomy
   — Hysterectomy
▪ Fertility issues

Uterine Prolapse, Cystocele, and Rectocele

- Preventive measures
  - Postpartum perineal exercises (Kegel's)
  - Spaced pregnancy
  - Weight control
- Differing S/S for each condition
- Surgical intervention
  - Hysterectomy, anterior and posterior vaginal repair
  - Pain management postop
  - Monitor urinary output postop
  - Observe for S/S of bleeding and infection postop

A client who had a vaginal hysterectomy the previous day is saturating perineal pads with blood and requires frequent changes during the night. What priority action should the nurse implement?
A. Provide iron-rich foods on each dietary tray
B. Monitor the client's vital signs every 2 hours
C. Administer IV fluids at the prescribed rate
D. Encourage postoperative leg exercises

Cancer of the Cervix

A human papillomavirus (HPV) is a papillomavirus that infects the skin and mucous membranes of humans. A vaccine is available that reduces the incidence of both cervical-related neoplasia and cervical cancer due to infection from HPV types 16 and 18. It is approved for females ages 9 to 26. It requires three shots over 6 months. Trade names for HPV vaccines: Gardasil and Cervarix
- Usually detected early with a Pap test
- Dysplasia treated with cryosurgery, laser, conization, possibly hysterectomy
- Early carcinoma treated with hysterectomy or intracavity radiation
- Late carcinoma treated with s beam radiation, chemotherapy, and/or pelvic exoneration

Care of the Client with Radiation Implants

- Client is NOT radioactive
- Implants do contain radioactivity
- Place in private room
- No pregnant caretakers or pregnant visitors
- Keep lead-lined container in the room
- All client secretions can be potentially radioactive
- Wear latex gloves when handling potentially contaminated secretions
- Wear radiation badge when providing care

1. Is the item written in a positive or a negative style?

2. Find the key words in the question.

3. Rephrase the question in your own words.

4. Rule out options:
   -
   -
   -

Ovarian Cancer

- Greatest risk factor is family history
- Asymptomatic in early stages
- Generalized feeling of abdominal fullness
- Sense of pelvic heaviness
- Loss of appetite
- Change in bowel habit
- Late stage symptoms
- Pelvic discomfort
- Low back pain
- Abdominal pain
- Ovarian cancer is the leading cause of death from gynecological cancers

Breast Cancer

- Risks
  - Family history
  - Age
  - Hyperestrogenism
  - Radiation exposure
- A great majority are discovered through breast self-exam
- Tumors tend to be in upper outer quadrant
  - Ductal carcinoma
  - Lobar carcinoma
  - Ductal carcinoma in situ
  - Inflammatory breast cancer (most aggressive)
  - Paget's disease (areola and nipple)
- Recommend mammogram every 1 to 2 years after age 40, then annual mammograms after age 50
- Treatment modalities
  - Surgical
    - Mastectomy
    - Modified radical mastectomy
    - Lumpectomy
    - Tissue expansion and breast implants
    - Musculocutaneous flap procedure
  - Radiation
  - Chemotherapy
  - Hormonal therapy
    - Tamoxifen (Nolvadex) blocks estrogen receptors
    - Fulvestrant (Faslodex) destroys estrogen receptors
    - Anastrozole (Arimidex), letrozole (Femara) prevents production of estrogen
  - Biological targeted therapies
  - Monoclonal antibodies

Nursing Assessment

- Hard lump not freely moveable
- Dimpling in skin
- Change in skin color
- Confirmed on mammogram and biopsy with frozen sections

Nursing Interventions

- Preoperative
  - Assess expectations
- Postoperative
  - Monitor for bleeding

— Position arm on operative side on a pillow
— No BP, IVs, or injections on operative side
— Provide emotional support, recognize the grieving process

Testicular Cancer

- Feeling of heaviness in lower abdomen
- Painless lump/swelling
- Postop orchiectomy
- Observe for bleeding
- Encourage genetic counseling (sperm banking)
- Postop management
  — Monitor for urine leaks
  — Avoid rectal manipulation
  — Low residue diet

Cancer of the Prostate

- Symptoms of urinary obstruction
- Elevated prostate-specific antigen (PSA)
- Surgical removal of the prostate
- Follow-up radiation and chemotherapy

Sexually Transmitted Diseases (STDs)

- Symptoms and treatment
  — Vary by disease
- Teach safer sex
  — Limit number of partners
  — Use latex condoms
- Report incidence of STDs to appropriate health agencies

Refer to Review Manuals for more in-depth information about STDs:

- *Evolve Reach Comprehensive Review for the NCLEX-RN Examination* (powered by HESI)
- *Mosby's Comprehensive Review of Nursing for NCLEX-RN Examination*
- *Saunders Comprehensive Review for the NCLEX-RN Examination*

The charge nurse is assigning rooms for four new clients, but only one private room is available on the oncology unit. Which client should be placed in the private room? The client with
A. Ovarian cancer receiving chemotherapy
B. Breast cancer receiving external beam radiation
C. Prostate cancer following transurethral resection
D. Cervical cancer with intracavity radiation

1. Is the item written in a positive or a negative style?

2. Find the key words in the question.

3. Rephrase the question in your own words.

4. Rule out options:
   ■
   ■
   ■

BURNS

A client is admitted to the emergency department with third-degree burns after running from a burning apartment. The client's voice is hoarse when he responds to the nurse's questions. What action should the nurse implement based on this finding?
A. Medicate with an anxiolytic agent
B. Administer an opiate via IV access
C. Provide tracheotomy set at bedside
D. Give oral ice chips upon request

1. Is the item written in a positive or a negative style?

2. Find the key words in the question.

3. Rephrase the question in your own words.

4. Rule out options:
   ■
   ■
   ■

Severity of Burn Depths

- First degree
  - Superficial
  - Partial thickness
  - Skin is pink or red
  - Painful
  - Slight swelling
- Second degree
  - Deep partial thickness
  - Painful
  - Red or white in color
  - Weeps fluid, blisters
  - Very edematous
  - Usually does not scar
- Third degree
  - Full thickness
  - Total destruction of dermis and epidermis
  - Requires skin grafting
  - Eschar develops

Determine Surface Area Burned

See figure on next page.

- Rule of Nines (adult)
  - Head and neck 9%
  - Each upper extremity 9%
  - Each lower extremity 18%
  - Front trunk 18%
  - Back trunk 18%
  - Perineal area 1%
- Rule of Nines (child over 9 years of age)
  - Head and neck 14%
  - Each upper extremity 9%
  - Each lower extremity 16%
  - Front trunk 18%
  - Back trunk 18%
- Rule of Nines (infant to 9 years old)
  - Head and neck 18%
  - Each upper extremity 9%
  - Each lower extremity 14%
  - Front trunk 18%
  - Back trunk 18%

Stages of Burn Care

- Stage 1—Emergent phase
  - Starts at time of injury
  - Lasts approximately 48 to 72 hours until capillary beds stabilize
  - Fluid shift from intravascular compartment to interstitial space
  - Causes shock!
- Stage II—Acute phase
  - Starts about 48 to 72 hours after burn
  - Diuresis begins
  - Fluid shifts from interstitial to intravascular
  - Watch for fluid overload
- Stage III—Rehabilitation phase
  - Begins after major wound closure has occurred
  - Grafting can occur
  - Depending on burn depth can take several years

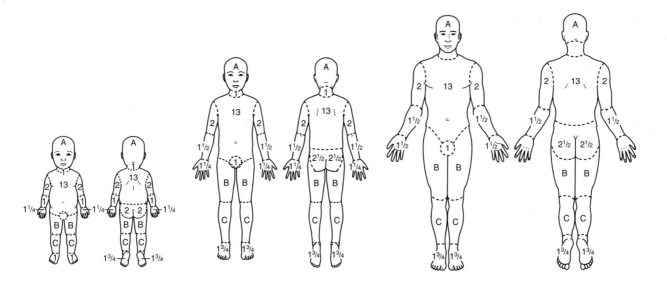

Relative percentages of areas affected by growth (age in years)

	0	1	5	10	15	Adult
A: Half of head	$9\frac{1}{2}$	$8\frac{1}{2}$	$6\frac{1}{2}$	$5\frac{1}{2}$	$4\frac{1}{2}$	$3\frac{1}{2}$
B: Half of thigh	$2\frac{3}{4}$	$3\frac{1}{4}$	4	$4\frac{1}{4}$	$4\frac{1}{2}$	$4\frac{3}{4}$
C: Half of leg	$2\frac{1}{2}$	$2\frac{1}{2}$	$2\frac{3}{4}$	3	$3\frac{1}{4}$	$3\frac{1}{2}$

Second degree _____ +
Third degree _____ =
Total percent burned _____

Nursing Assessment

- Assess the ABCs
  — Airway
  — Breathing
  — Circulation
- Assess for S/S of adequate hydration
- S/S of inhalation burns
- Bowel sounds
- Urinary output

Nursing Plans and Interventions

- Thermal burn—remove clothing, immerse burns in tepid water, apply sterile dressing
- Chemical burns—flush with water or saline
- Electrical burns—separate client from electrical source
- Maintain airway, breathing, circulation
- Pain management with IV pain medication

Fluid Management

- Fluid replacement is calculated using a variety of formulas
- Formula is based on extent of the burn, client's body weight, and depth of the burn
- In the first 24 hours, the fluid replacement is normally very large (e.g., 5000 mL in first 8 hours)

A newly licensed nurse is preparing to perform wound care for a burn client for the first time. What is the most important action to implement before wound care?

A. Explain step-by-step wound care
B. Obtain all needed supplies
C. Hang the next scheduled IV antibiotic
D. Determine time of last analgesia

Medications for Burns

- Antimicrobial agents
  — Silver sulfadiazine (Silvadene, Flamazine)
  — Mafenide acetate (Sulfamylon)
  — Silver-impregnated dressings (Acticoat, Silverlon, Aquacel Ag)
- Analgesia
  — Morphine
  — All analgesic drugs
  — Sustained-release morphine (MS Contin)
  — Hydromorphone (Dilaudid)
  — Fentanyl (Sublimaze)
  — Oxycodone (contained in Percocet)
  — Methadone
  — Nonsteroidal anti-inflammatory (e.g., ketoprofen [Orudis])
  — Adjuvant analgesics (e.g., gabapentin)
- Nutritional Support
  — Vitamins A, C, E, and multivitamins
  — Minerals: zinc, iron (ferrous sulfate)
  — Oxandrolone (Oxandrin)
- Sedation
  — Haloperidol (Haldol)
  — Lorazepam (Ativan)
  — Midazolam (Versed)
- Gastrointestinal Support
  — Ranitidine (Zantac)
  — Nystatin (Mycostatin)
  — Mylanta, Maalox

Wound Care

- Dressing changes are very painful! Medicate client prior to procedure
- Apply silver sulfadiazine (Silvadene cream) to burns as prescribed

1. Is the item written in a positive or a negative style?

2. Find the key words in the question.

3. Rephrase the question in your own words.

4. Rule out options:
   -
   -
   -

What is the best snack to provide a client during the acute stage of burn management?
A. Applesauce and beef broth
B. Peanut butter sandwich and milkshake
C. Pretzels and fruit juice
D. Chocolate cookies and coffee

1. Is the item written in a positive or a negative style?

2. Find the key words in the question.

3. Rephrase the question in your own words.

4. Rule out options:
   ▪
   ▪
   ▪

6 | Pediatric Nursing

The nurse directs the unlicensed assistive personnel (UAP) to play with a 4-year-old child on bed rest. Which activity should the nurse recommend?
A. Monopoly board game
B. Looking at picture books
C. Fifty-piece puzzle
D. Hand puppets

GROWTH AND DEVELOPMENT

- The five major developmental periods
  — Prenatal
  — Infancy
  — Early childhood
  — Middle childhood
  — Later childhood (pubescence and adolescence)
- The developmental theories most widely used in explaining child growth and development:
  — Freud's psychosexual stages
  — Erikson's stages of psychosocial development
  — Piaget's stages of cognitive development
  — Kohlberg's stages of moral development
- Through play, children learn about their world and how to relate to things, people, and situations. Play provides a means of development in the areas of
  — Sensorimotor activity
  — Intellectual progress
  — Socialization
  — Creativity
  — Self-awareness
  — Moral behavior
  — Release of tension
  — Expression of emotions

Normal Growth and Development
Know norms for growth and development!
- Toddlers (1-3 years)
  — Throws ball overhand at 18 months
  — Two- to three-word sentences at 2 years
  — Toilet training starts around 2 years
  — Toddlers are ritualistic
  — No concept of time
  — Frequent tantrums
- Preschool (3-5 years)
  — Rides tricycle at 3 years
  — Favorite word: WHY?
  — Car seat safety: under 4 years, 40 lb, and 40 inches
  — Sentences of 5 to 8 words

1. Is the item written in a positive or a negative style?

2. Find the key words in the question.

3. Rephrase the question in your own words.

4. Rule out options:
   - ▪
   - ▪
   - ▪

HESI Hint
NCLEX Focus Questions
- Know norms for growth and development!
  — Birth weight doubles by 6 months, triples by 12 months
  — Plays "peek-a-boo" by 6 months
  — Sits upright without support by 8 months
  — Fine pincer grasp by 10 to 12 months (can pick up Cheerios)

- School age (6-12 years)
  — Each year gains 4 to 6 lb, grows 2 inches
  — Learns to tell time
  — Socialization with peers very important
- Adolescence (12-19 years)
  — Rapid growth second only to first year of life!
  — Secondary sex characteristics develop
  — More concerned about scars than medical diagnosis

PAIN ASSESSMENT AND MANAGEMENT

- Assessment is based upon verbal report from child and nonverbal behavior, and includes parents' information.
- Use pain scale appropriate to child's development.
- Safety is a major priority for administering medication.
- Make sure dose is SAFE for age and weight.

CHILD HEALTH PROMOTION

- Immunizations
- Communicable diseases
- Poisoning

Immunization Teaching

- Common cold does NOT contraindicate getting immunization unless fever >99 ° F
- Normal to have fever <102 ° F, redness and soreness at site 2 to 3 days after injection
- Call MD if high-pitched crying, seizures, or high fever occur
- Use acetaminophen orally q 4-6 hr (10-15 mg/kg)

Communicable Diseases

- The incidence of common childhood communicable diseases has declined greatly since the advent of immunizations, but they do occur and nurses should be able to identify the infection.
  — Measles—Signs and symptoms (S/S) are photophobia, Koplik's spots on buccal mucosa, and rash that begins on face and spreads downward.
  — Rubeola
  — Rubella
  — Roseola
  — Mumps
  — Pertussis
  — Chickenpox—Lesions begin on trunk and spread to face; infection is noncommunicable after scabs form.
  — Diphtheria
  — Erythema infectiosum (fifth disease)
- Treat fever from infection with acetaminophen not ASA (acetylsalicylic acid, aspirin).
- Isolation is required during the infectious phase of the infection.

HESI Hint
NCLEX Question Focus
- Use knowledge from the immunization chart: www.cdc.gov/vaccines/recs/schedules/
- Childhood immunization
  — Example: What would be the vaccines the nurse would expect to be prescribed for a 2-month-old brought into the pediatrician's office for a well checkup? DTaP, HepB, HIB, IPV, and PCV
  — Example: Withhold MMR vaccine for person with history of anaphylactic reaction to neomycin or eggs.

- Teaching is the primary intervention for prevention of spread.
- Supportive measures are given while the disease runs its course.

Poisonings

- Frequent cause of childhood injury—teach poison-proof methods for the home!
- GI disturbance is a common symptom
- Burns of mouth, pharynx with caustic poisonings
- Identify poisonous agent quickly!
- Do the ABCs
- Syrup of ipecac is NO LONGER recommended:
  — Teach parents to not make the child vomit by any means, as it may cause more damage
  — Call Poison Control Center or 911, based on how the child is acting

The nurse is performing an initial assessment of a 2-year-old child with suspected bacterial epiglottitis. What assessment is needed?
A. Use a tongue depressor to assess for erythema
B. Obtain a throat swab for culture and sensitivity
C. Observe for the presence of drooling
D. Measure pain using a FACES scale

1. Is the item written in a positive or a negative style?

2. Find the key words in the question.

3. Rephrase the question in your own words.

4. Rule out options:
   ■
   ■
   ■

RESPIRATORY DYSFUNCTION

- Respiratory dysfunction
  — Infection of the respiratory tract
  — Croup syndromes
  — Tuberculosis
  — Asthma
  — Cystic fibrosis

  — Passive inhalation of tobacco smoke contributes to respiratory illness in children.

Respiratory Infections
- Nasopharyngitis
- Tonsillitis
  — May be viral or bacterial
  —Treatment important if related to streptococcal infection
  — Check prothrombin time (PT) and partial thromboplastin time (PTT) prior to surgery
  — Soft foods and oral fluids
  — Do not use straws
  — Monitor for bleeding
  — Highest risk for bleeding is during first 24 hours and 5 to 10 days postop

HESI Hint
Respiratory Disorders
- Be familiar with normal values for respiratory and pulse rates for children.
- Know cardinal and other signs of respiratory distress.
- Respiratory failure will usually occur before cardiac failure.

- Otitis media
  - S/S: fever, pulling at ear
  - Discharge from ear
  - Administer antibiotics
  - Reduce body temperature to prevent febrile seizures

- Bacterial tracheitis
- Bronchitis
- Respiratory syncytial virus (RSV)/bronchiolitis
  - Isolate the child (contact isolation)
  - Nurse caring for children with RSV should not care for other children
  - Monitor respiratory status
  - Antiviral agent (ribavirin aerosols)
  - Maintain patent airway

- Epiglottitis
  - S/S: high fever, sore throat, muffled voice, tripod position
  - Hib vaccine for prevention
  - IV antibiotics
  - Do not examine throat—may cause complete airway obstruction

Asthma

- The leading cause of chronic illness in children
- Allergies influence persistence and severity
- Complex disorder involving biochemical, immunologic, infections, endocrine and psychological factors.
- Nursing assessment and interventions
  - S/S: tight cough, expiratory wheezing, peak flow levels
  - Monitor closely for respiratory distress, need for O_2 nebulizer therapy

Cystic Fibrosis (CF)

- Most frequently occurring inherited disease of Caucasian children
- Transmitted by an autosomal recessive gene located on chromosome 7 (inherit from both parents)
- Diagnosis of CF may be based on a number of criteria
  - Family history
  - Absence of pancreatic enzymes
    - Steatorrhea
  - Chronic pulmonary involvement
    - Goal is to prevent respiratory infections

— Administer pancreatic enzymes with each meal and snacks
— Administer fat-soluble vitamins
— Teach family percussion and postural drainage techniques
— Laboratory identification of CF mutations
— Positive newborn screening test
  • First sign may be meconium ileus at birth
— Abnormally high sweat chloride concentration (pilocarpine test or sweat test)
— Delayed growth—poor weight gain

CARDIOVASCULAR DISORDERS

Congenital Heart Disorders
■ May be classified as:
— Acyanotic: ventricular septal defect, atrial septal defect, patent ductus arteriosus, coarctation of the aorta, aortic stenosis
— Cyanotic: tetralogy of Fallot, truncus arteriosus, transposition of the great vessels

Ventricular Septal Defect (VSD)
■ Hole between ventricles
■ May close spontaneously
■ L → R shunt

For illustrations of cardiovascular disorders, see a textbook or an NCLEX Review Manual:
■ *Evolve Reach Comprehensive Review for the NCLEX-RN Examination* (powered by HESI)
■ *Mosby's Comprehensive Review of Nursing for NCLEX-RN Examination*
■ *Saunders Comprehensive Review for the NCLEX-RN Examination*

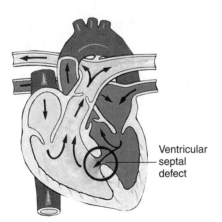

Ventricular septal defect

Atrial Septal Defects (ASD)

- L → R shunt
- Abnormal opening in the septum between the left and right atria

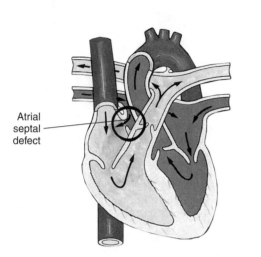

Atrial septal defect

Patent Ductus Arteriosus (PDA)

- Allows oxygenated blood pumped into aorta from left ventricle to return to the lungs
- Large PDAs allow excess blood into the lungs, leading to pulmonary hypertension

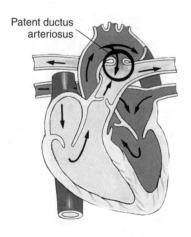

Patent ductus arteriosus

Coarctation of the Aorta

- Obstructive disorder
- Usually just past left subclavian artery
- Significant decrease in blood flow to abdomen and legs; majority of blood shunted to head and arms

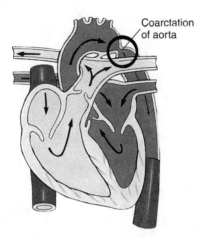

Coarctation of aorta

Aortic Stenosis

- Obstruction of blood flow from the ventricles
- S/S related to ↓ cardiac output

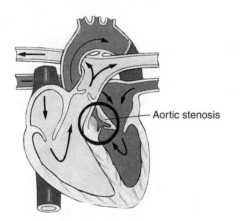

Aortic stenosis

Tetralogy of Fallot

- Four defects: pulmonary stenosis, ventricular septal defect, overriding aorta, right ventricle hypertrophy
- Unoxygenated blood is pumped into systemic system

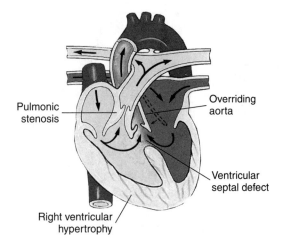

Pulmonic stenosis

Overriding aorta

Ventricular septal defect

Right ventricular hypertrophy

Truncus Arteriosus

- Pulmonary artery and aorta do not separate
- Blood from both vessels mix, resulting in cyanosis

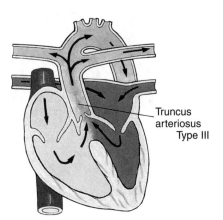

Truncus arteriosus Type III

- **Transposition of the Great Vessels**
- O_2 circulates through left side of heart to lungs and back to left side
- Unoxygenated blood enters right atrium from body, goes to right ventricle and back out to body
- Incompatible with life unless VSD, ASD, and/or PDA present

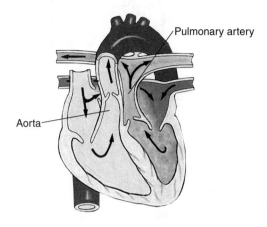

Pulmonary artery

Aorta

Nursing Interventions

- Maintain nutritional status, feeding should not last >30 min
- Plan frequent rest periods
- Administer digoxin, diuretics and angiotensin-converting enzyme (ACE) inhibitors as prescribed
- Cardiac catheterization probable intervention
  — Know risks of cardiac catheterization
  — Know postcatheterization assessment parameters
  — Provide age-appropriate teaching for children

Congestive Heart Failure

- Common complication of congenital heart disorders
- S/S: pedal edema (face and eyes of infant), neck vein distention, cyanosis, grunting
- Monitor vital signs (VS), elevate head of bed, O_2 as ordered
- Administer digoxin, diuretics, and ACE inhibitors
- Weigh daily on same scale

Managing Digoxin Therapy in Children

- Must take child's apical pulse prior to administration
- Hold in infants <100 beats/min, children <80 beats/ min
- Do not skip or try to make up doses
- Give 1 to 2 hours before meals
- Watch for S/S of toxicity and teach parents
  — Vomiting, anorexia, diarrhea, muscle weakness, drowsiness
- Watch K^+ level, especially if on diuretics

Rheumatic Fever
- Peaks in school-age children
- Most common cause of acquired heart disease
- Affects connective tissue
- S/S: sore throat, appears to be getting better, then fever develops along with rash, chorea, elevated erythrocyte sedimentation rate (ESR)

Nursing Care Management
- Encourage compliance with drug regimens
  - Penicillin remains the drug of choice.
  - Salicylates are used to control the inflammatory process, especially in the joints, and to reduce fever and discomfort.
  - Administration of prednisone may be indicated in some patients with heart failure.
- Facilitate recovery from the illness
  - Traditionally, bed rest or at least limited activity has been recommended during the acute illness.
- Provide emotional support
- Prevent recurrence of the disease
  - Secondary prevention involves monthly intramuscular injections of benzathine penicillin G, two daily oral doses of penicillin V, or one daily dose of sulfadiazine sulfisoxazole or erythromycin.

The nurse reviews the medication record of a 2-month-old and notes that the infant was given a scheduled dose of digoxin with a documented apical pulse of 76 beats/min. What action should the nurse take first?
A. Assess the current apical heart rate
B. Observe for the onset of diarrhea
C. Complete an adverse occurrence report
D. Determine the serum potassium level

1. Is the item written in a positive or a negative style?

2. Find the key words in the question.

3. Rephrase the question in your own words.

4. Rule out options:
   -
   -
   -

A child with hydrocephalus is 1 day postoperative for revision of a ventriculoatrial shunt. Which finding is most important?
A. Increased blood pressure
B. Increased temperature
C. Increased serum glucose
D. Increased hematocrit

1. Is the item written in a positive or a negative style?

2. Find the key words in the question.

3. Rephrase the question in your own words.

4. Rule out options:
   -
   -
   -

NEUROMUSCULAR DISORDERS

Down Syndrome

- Trisomy 21
- Flat, broad nasal bridge; upward, outward slant of eyes
- Commonly associated problems
  — Cardiac defects
  — Delayed development
  — Respiratory problems

Cerebral Palsy (CP)

- Diagnosis made on evaluation of child
  — Persistent neonatal reflexes after 6 months
  — Spasticity
  — Scissoring of legs
  — Tight abductor muscles of hips
  — Tightening of heel cord
  — No parachute reflex to protect self from falling
  — Prevent aspiration with feedings
  — Administer phenytoin (Dilantin) for seizures
  — Administer diazepam (Valium) for muscle spasms

Spina Bifida Occulta

- No sac present
- Suspect if tuft of hair at base of spine

Meningocele

- Contains only meninges and spinal fluid
- No nerves are in spinal sac

Myelomeningocele

- Sac contains spinal fluid, meninges, and nerves
- Will have sensory and motor defects
- Preop/postop care:
  — Monitor urine output
  — Watch for ↑ ICP
  — Keep sac free of stool/urine
  — Measure head circumference q 8 hr and check fontanels

Hydrocephalus

- Abnormal accumulation of cerebrospinal fluid (CSF)
- Symptoms
  — ↑ Intracranial pressure (ICP)
  — ↑ BP
  — ↓ Pulse
  — Changes in level of consciousness (LOC)
  — Irritability and vomiting
- Interventions
  — Elevate head of bed
  — Seizure precautions
  — Prepare for shunt placement
    • Assess for shunt malfunctioning
    • Monitor for S/S of infection
  — Teaching related to shunt replacement
    • Surgeries will continue as the child grows

HESI Hint

- NCLEX-RN questions are likely to relate to supporting the child/parent to achieve the highest level of functioning.
  — Always evaluate mental age
  — Feed to back and side of mouth due to tongue thrust
  — Refer family to early intervention program

Seizures

- More common in children under 2 years
- Types of seizures
  - Generalized tonic/clonic
    - Grand mal seizure with loss of consciousness
    - Aura precedes seizure
    - Tonic phase — stiffness of body
    - Clonic phase — spasms and relaxation
    - Postictal phase — sleepy and disoriented
  - Petit mal
    - Momentary loss of consciousness, appears like daydreaming
    - Lasts 5 to 10 sec
  - Absence
  - Myoclonic
  - Partial
  - Infantile spasms

Nursing Plans and Interventions for Seizures

- Maintain patent airway
- Side rails up
- Pad side rails
- Do not put tongue blade in the mouth
- Administer anticonvulsants
  - Different types of seizures require specific anticonvulsants
- Teach family/client to administer the medications correctly.

Anticonvulsants and Types of Seizures

- Phenobarbital
  - Generalized tonic-clonic
  - Partial
  - Status epilepticus
- Primidone (Mysoline)
  - Generalized tonic-clonic
  - Partial
- Phenytoin (Dilantin)
  - Generalized tonic-clonic
  - Partial
  - Status epilepticus
- Valproic acid (Depakene)
  - Generalized tonic-clonic
  - Absence
  - Myoclonic
  - Partial
- Clonazepam (Rivotril)
  - Absence
  - Myoclonic
  - Infantile spasms
  - Partial
- Carbamazepine (Tegretol)
  - Generalized tonic-clonic
  - Partial

Bacterial Meningitis

- Usually caused by *Streptococcus pneumoniae* and less often by *Haemophilus influenzae*, type B (Hib) vaccine (due to use of Hib vaccination)
- Signs and symptoms
  - Older children: include S/S of increased ICP, neck stiffness, + Kernig's sign, + Brudzinski's sign
  - Infants: classic signs absent, poor feeding, vomiting, irritability, bulging fontanels
- Diagnostic procedures include lumbar puncture for laboratory analysis
- Interventions
  - Isolate at least 24 hours
  - Administer antibiotics
  - Frequent VS and neurological checks
    - Increased ICP, muscle twitching, and changes in LOC
  - Measure head circumference daily in infants
  - SIADH (syndrome of inappropriate antidiuretic hormone) occurs frequently
    - Fluid restrictions may be necessary

AGE	ORGANISM
Birth to 2 months	Enteric bacilli
	Group B streptococci
2 months to 12 years	*H. influenzae* type b
	Streptococcus pneumoniae
	Neisseria meningitidis (meningococci)
12 years and older	*N. meningitidis*
	S. pneumoniae

Reye Syndrome

- Etiology often, but NOT ALWAYS, associated with aspirin use and influenza or varicella
- Rapidly progressing encephalopathy
- S/S: lethargy progressing to coma, vomiting, hypoglycemia
- Frequent neurological checks, maintain airway
- Mannitol for ICP control
- Early diagnosis is important to improve client outcome

Brain Tumors

- Second most common cancer in children
- Treatment
  - Surgery
  - Radiation
  - Chemotherapy
- Common symptoms
  - Early morning headache relieved by vomiting
  - Nystagmus
  - Incoordination (clumsy)
- Postoperative

- If large tumor removed, the child is not placed on the operative side
- Follow seizure precautions
- Prevent ↑ ICP
- Prepare family for appearance of child

Muscular Dystrophy (MD)

- Duchenne MD
  - Onset between ages 2 and 6 years
  - Is the most severe and most common MD of childhood
  - X-linked recessive disorder
- Diagnosis
  - Muscle biopsy muscle fibers degenerate and replaced by connective tissue and fat
  - Electromyogram (EMG) shows decreased muscle function
  - Serum creatine phosphokinase (CK) levels are extremely high in the first 2 years of life before the onset
- Symptoms
  - Delayed walking
  - Frequent falls
  - Easily tires when walking
- Interventions
  - Exercise
  - Prevent falls
  - Assistive devices for ambulation

RENAL DISORDERS IN CHILDREN

Common inflammatory disorders are urinary tract infection, nephrotic syndrome, and acute glomerulonephritis.

Urinary Tract Infection (UTI)

- More common in girls
- Symptoms
  - Poor food intake
  - Strong-smelling urine
  - Fever
  - Pain with urination
- Interventions
  - Obtain urine culture before starting antibiotics
  - Teach home care:
    - Finish all antibiotics
    - Avoid bubble baths
    - Increase intake of acidic fluids, such as apple or cranberry juice

Vesicoureteral Reflux

- Retrograde flow of bladder urine into the ureters
- May see in child with myelomeningocele
- Symptoms
  - Recurrent UTIs
  - Common with neurogenic bladder
- Interventions
  - Teach to prevent UTI
  - Record output after catheterization
  - Maintain hydration

HESI Hint
Review medications used with renal disorders.

Acute Glomerulonephritis (AGN)

- Common features
  - Oliguria
  - Edema
  - Hypertension
  - Circulatory congestion
  - Hematuria
  - Proteinuria
- Therapeutic management
  - Maintenance of fluid balance
  - Treatment of hypertension
- Assessment
  - Recent strep infection
  - Dark urine "iced tea"
  - Irritable and/or lethargic
  - Symptoms of
    - Hypovolemic shock
    - CHF
- Interventions
  - VS q 4 hr
  - Daily weights
  - Low-sodium, low-potassium diet

Nephrotic Syndrome

Characterized by increased glomerular permeability to protein

- Management
  - Reducing excretion of protein
  - Reducing or preventing fluid retention by tissues
  - Preventing infection and other complications
- Assessment
  - Frothy urine
  - Massive proteinuria
  - Edema
  - Anorexia
- Intervention
  - Skin care
  - Administer medications
- Diuretics
- Corticosteroid therapy
- Immunosuppressants
  - Small frequent feeding
  - Dietary control
- Discharge teaching
  - Daily weights
  - Side effects of meds
  - Prevent infections

Acute Renal Failure Management

- Treatment of the underlying cause
- Managing the complications of renal failure
- Providing supportive therapy

Abnormalities in Chronic Renal Failure

- Waste product retention
- Water and sodium retention
- Hyperkalemia
- Acidosis

- Calcium and phosphorus disturbance
- Anemia
- Hypertension
- Growth disturbances

Home Dialysis
- Nursing interventions
  — Educate the family about
    - The disease, its implications, the therapeutic plan
    - Possible psychological effects of the disease
    - Treatment and technical aspects of the procedure
- Major concerns in kidney transplantation
  — Tissue matching
  — Prevention of rejection
  — Psychological concerns
- Self-image related to body changes from corticosteroid therapy

Hypospadias
- Congenital defect
- Symptoms
  — Altered urinary stream
  — Ventral curvature of penis
  — Undescended testes
- Interventions
  — Surgical correction before preschool age
  — Postop circulation checks to penis
  — Monitor Foley drainage
  — Teach home care for catheter
  — Increase oral fluids

Wilms' Tumor
- Usually encapsulated
- Good prognosis with early detection
- Do NOT palpate abdomen
- Postop care
  — Monitor BP
  — Urine output
  — Nasogastric (NG) tube
  — Monitor bowel sounds

The nurse is planning care for an infant with a tracheoesophageal fistula. Which nursing diagnosis has the highest priority?
A. Infection, risk for
B. Injury, risk for
C. Nutrition, altered, less than
D. Aspiration, risk for

1. **Is the item written in a positive or a negative style?**

2. **Find the key words in the question.**

3. **Rephrase the question in your own words.**

4. **Rule out options:**
   -
   -
   -

GASTROINTESTINAL DISORDERS

Nutritional Assessment

- Present nutritional status
- Body mass index
- Dietary history (information from parents)
- Past nutrition assessment
- Height
- Weight
- Head circumference
- Skinfold thickness
- Arm circumference
- Iron deficiency most common in children 12 to 36 months and adolescent females
  — May need $FeSO_4$ drops—use straw, give with orange juice, do not give with dairy foods

Diarrhea

- Worldwide leading cause of death in children < 5 years of age
- Classified as acute or chronic
- Common problem for infants
- Nursing management goals
  — Assessment of the fluid and electrolyte imbalance
    • Monitor I & O
    • Calculate fluid replacement and maintenance needs
  — Rehydration
  — Maintenance fluid therapy
  — Reintroduction of adequate diet
  — Do not give antidiarrheal agents to children
- Symptoms
  — Depressed sunken eyes
  — Weight loss
  — Decreased urine output

Cleft Lip or Cleft Palate

- Malformation of the face or oral cavity
- Initial closure of cleft lip is performed when infant weighs ~10lb
- Closure of cleft palate at around 1 year
- Promote bonding
- Breck/Habermann feeder
- Maintain airway
- No straws, no spoons, only soft foods for cleft palate

Pyloric Stenosis

- Common in first-born males
- Vomiting becomes projectile around day 14 after birth

- Preop
  - — Assess for dehydration
  - — Weigh daily
  - — Small frequent feedings
- Postop
  - — Small, frequent feedings
  - — Position on right side, semi-Fowler's position
  - — Burp frequently
  - — Weigh daily

Intussusception

- Telescoping of one part of intestine
- Emergency intervention is needed (barium enema, or abdominal surgery)

Congenital Aganglionic Megacolon (Hirschsprung's Disease)

- Series of surgeries to correct
- Temporary colostomy

Anorectal Malformations

- Congenital malformations
- S/S: unusual-appearing anal dimple, does not pass meconium stool in first 24 hours, meconium in urine or from perineal fistula
- Teach home care for temporary colostomy

HEMATOLOGICAL DISORDERS

Iron Deficiency Anemia

- Common in infants, toddlers, and adolescent females Review Hgb norms for children
- Teach family about administering oral iron

Sickle Cell Anemia

- Autosomal recessive disorder
  - — Fetal Hgb does not sickle
- Hydration to promote hemodilution
- Symptoms
  - — Crisis
    - • Fever and pain
- Keep well hydrated
- Do not give supplemental iron
- Give folic acid orally

Hemophilia

- X-linked recessive disorder
- Interventions
  — Administer fresh frozen plasma
  — Apply pressure to even minor bleeds
  — Increased risk for bleeding with growth and development stages

Acute Lymphocytic Leukemia

- Symptoms
  — Pallor
  — Petechiae
  — Infections
  — Bone joint pain
  — Enlarged lymph nodes
- Interventions
  — Reverse isolation
  — Give blood products as ordered
  — Administer chemotherapeutic agents
  — Emotional support to patient and family

METABOLIC AND ENDOCRINE DISORDERS

Phenylketonuria (PKU)

- Autosomal recessive disorder
- Newborn screening with Guthrie test
  — Positive (+) when serum phenylalanine is 4 mg/dL
  — Done at birth and at 3 weeks
- Strict adherence to low-phenylalanine diet
- Special PKU formula
- Avoid meat, milk, dairy, and eggs
- Use: fruits, juices, cereal, bread, and starches
- Must follow diet until brain growth complete and with any pregnancy (if female)

Insulin-Dependent Diabetes Mellitus

- Common in school-age children
- Cognitive level and age should be considered when planning teaching
- Regular IV insulin with ketoacidosis
- Dietary teaching
- Exercise management
- Insulin administration

HESI Hint

Common NCLEX questions may focus on ability to explain transmission patterns.

HESI Hint

Be aware that type 2 diabetes has been increasing in children in relation to obesity, lack of exercise, and family history of type 2 diabetes.

SKELETAL DISORDERS

Nursing Assessment

- 5 Ps may indicate ischemia
  - Pain
  - Pallor
  - Paresthesia
  - Pulselessness
  - Paralysis
- Visible signs of fractures
- Obtain baseline pulses, color, movement, sensation, temperature, swelling, and pain
- Report any changes immediately

Traction

- Buck's traction
  - For knee immobilization
- Russell traction
  - For fracture of femur or lower leg
- Dunlap's traction
  - Can be skeletal or skin
- 90°/90° traction
- Provide appropriate play toys, teach cast care to family, prevent cast soilage with diapering

Congenital Dislocated Hip

- Assessment
  - Positive Ortolani sign
  - Unequal fold of skin on buttocks and thigh
  - Limited abduction of hip
- Intervention
  - Apply Pavlik harness
    - Abduction device worn 24 hr/day
- Surgical correction
  - Postop intervention
    - Hip spica cast care

Scoliosis

- S-shaped curvature of the spine.
- Most common nontraumatic skeletal condition in children.
- Scoliosis affects both genders at any age, but it is most commonly seen in adolescents.
- Curvatures in adolescent girls seem to progress faster and require treatment more frequently than those in boys

Juvenile Rheumatoid Arthritis (JRA)

- Juvenile rheumatoid arthritis is the most common arthritic condition of childhood.
- These inflammatory diseases involve the joints, connective tissues, and viscera.
- The exact cause is unknown, but infections and an autoimmune response have been implicated.
- Therapy consists of administration of medications, such as NSAIDs, methotrexate, or aspirin, along with exercise, heat application, and support of joints.

The LPN is assigned to care for a 3-year-old with Reye syndrome. The child's temperature is 102.4° F, and the LPN is preparing to administer aspirin PO. What action should the charge nurse implement?

A. Direct the LPN to assess the gag reflex and LOC

B. Advise the LPN to wait until the fever is greater than 102.4° F

C. Remind the LPN to hold all aspirin-containing medication

D. Tell the LPN to notify the healthcare provider

1. Is the item written in a positive or a negative style?

2. Find the key words in the question.

3. Rephrase the question in your own words.

4. Rule out options:
   -
   -
   -

A 36-week gestational client is placed in the lithotomy position and suddenly complains of feeling breathless and lightheaded, and exhibits marked pallor. What action should the nurse implement first?
A. Turn to a lateral position
B. Place in Trendelenburg position
C. Place the client's legs flat
D. Initiate distraction techniques

ANATOMY AND PHYSIOLOGY OF REPRODUCTION

The Menstrual Cycle

- Menstrual phase
  — 1 to 5 days
  — No hormones secreted
  — Endometrial shedding (50-60 mL)
- Proliferative (follicular) phase
  — Day 5 to ovulation
  — Estrogen, follicle-stimulating hormone (FSH), and luteinizing hormone (LH) secreted
  — Endometrium restored
  — Ovulation begins
- Secretory (luteal) phase
  — Ovulation to about 3 days before menstruation
  — Estrogen levels off
  — Progesterone increases
  — Uterus ready to accept fertilized embryo
- Ischemic phase
  — If fertilization does not occur, corpus luteum degenerates
  — Estrogen and progesterone drop sharply
  — Endometrium becomes ischemic
  — Uterus sheds lining as menstrual blood

Fetal/Maternal Changes

- Review the charts focusing on maternal physiologic changes and the nursing interventions that go along with those changes
- Understanding fetal development will help when you try to answer "parent teaching" NCLEX questions

1. Is the item written in a positive or a negative style?

2. Find the key words in the question.

3. Rephrase the question in your own words.

4. Rule out options:
   - ■
   - ■
   - ■

HESI Hints

- Ovulation occurs 14 days before the first day of the next menstrual cycle.
  — If the woman has a 28-day cycle, that is halfway between periods.
  — However, if her cycle is shorter or longer, it will not be at the halfway point!
- Sperm live about 3 days and eggs about 24 hours.
- Fertilization usually takes place in the ampulla of the fallopian tube.
- It takes 7 to 10 days from fertilization to the time implantation is completed.
- Pregnancy is divided into three trimesters (13 weeks each).

Psychosocial Adaptation

- First trimester: Ambivalence is NORMAL even in planned and/or desired pregnancies.
- Second trimester: Pregnancy becomes more real and ambivalence wanes.
- Third trimester: Woman becomes more introverted and focused on the baby.
- Throughout pregnancy: Mood swings are common.

Assess for Violence

- Battering, emotional or physical abuse can begin with pregnancy
- Assess for abuse in private, away from the male partner
- Nurse needs to know
  — Local resources
  — How to determine safety of client

Gravidity and Parity

- Gravida: number of times one has been pregnant regardless of outcome
- Para: number of deliveries (not children) occurring after 20 weeks of gestation
  — Multiple births count as one
  — Pregnancy loss before 20 weeks counted as abortion but add 1 to gravidity
  — Fetal demise after 20 weeks is added to parity
- TPAL equals number of
  — Term pregnancies
  — Preterm pregnancies
  — Abortions (elective or spontaneous)
  — Living children

Estimated Date of Birth (EDB)

Nagele's Rule

- Count back 3 months from date of last normal menstrual period
- Add 1 year and 7 days
- Example: If the last menstrual period was May 2, 2008, EDB would be February 9, 2009

Vital Signs and Laboratory Values

- BP: raise no more than 30 points systolic and 15 points diastolic
- Pulse: average 60 to 90 beats/min
- Respirations: 16 to 24 breaths/min
- Temperature: 97° to 100° F
- Hemoglobin: >11 g/dL
- Hematocrit: >33%

Fundal Height

- At 12 to 13 weeks: fundus rises out of symphysis
- At 20 weeks: fundus at umbilicus
- From 24 weeks to about 36 weeks: fundal height (measured in cm) from the symphysis is equal to number of weeks of gestation if it is a single pregnancy

Anticipatory Guidance

- First trimester
  — Discomforts usually subside by 13 weeks
  — Need 8 hours sleep and planned rest periods
  — May exercise as long as can converse easily while exercising
  — Bathe until membranes rupture
  — Travel
    - Car—take frequent breaks and wear seatbelts
    - Airplane—keep well hydrated and move frequently
  — No medications, alcohol, or smoking
- Second trimester
  — Sexual needs/desires may change, encourage communication with partner
  — Regular check-ups/dental hygiene
  — Delay major x-rays and dental work if possible
- Third trimester
  — Childbirth classes
  — Urinary frequency and dyspnea return
  — Safety and balance
  — Round ligament pain
  — Come to hospital when contractions are regular and 5 minutes apart
  — Risks and symptoms of premature labor

Nutrition

- Assessment
  — 24-hour diet recall
  — Determine individual deficiencies
  — Determine BMI for status of risk of over- or underweight
- Needs during pregnancy increase:
  — Calories: 300/day above basal and activity needs
  — Protein: 60 g/day
  — Iron: 30+ mg/day
  — Folic acid: 800 to 1000 mcg/day
  — Vitamin A: 770 to 750 mcg
  — Vitamin C: 80 to 85 mg
  — Calcium: 1200 mg/day
  — Fluid intake: 8 to 10 glasses/day (4 to 6 should be water)

HESI Hint

Know how to calculate the body mass index (BMI):

$$BMI = Weight \div Height^2$$

where weight is in kilograms and height is in meters

WEIGHT LEVEL BEFORE PREGNANCY	TOTAL GAIN DURING PREGNANCY	TOTAL GAIN IN FIRST TRIMESTER	WEEKLY GAIN IN SECOND AND THIRD TRIMESTERS
Normal weight (BMI 19.8-26.0)	11.5-16 kg (25-35 lb)	1.6 kg (3.5 lb)	0.44 kg (0.97 lb)
Underweight (BMI <19.8)	12.5-18 kg (28-40 lb)	2.3 kg (5 lb)	0.49 kg (1.07 lb)
Overweight (BMI >26, <29)	7-11 kg (15-25 lb)	0.9 kg (2 lb)	0.3 kg (0.67 lb)
Obese (BMI >29)	At least 6.8 kg (15 lb)	Individually determined	Individually determined
Twin pregnancy	16-20.5 kg (35-45 lb)	1.6 kg (3.5 lb)	0.75 kg (1.5 lb)

A female client has her suspected pregnancy confirmed. The client tells the nurse she had one pregnancy that she delivered at 39 weeks, twins that she delivered at 34 weeks, and a single gestation that she delivered at 35 weeks. Using the TPAL notation, how should the nurse record the client's gravidity and parity?

A. 3-0-3-0-3
B. 3-1-1-1-3
C. 4-1-2-0-4
D. 4-2-1-0-3

1. Is the item written in a positive or a negative style?

2. Find the key words in the question.

3. Rephrase the question in your own words.

4. Rule out options:
   ■
   ■
   ■

Ultrasonography

Uses:

■ In first trimester to determine
— Number of fetuses
— Presence or absence of cardiac activity
— Uterine abnormalities
— Gestational age assessment
— As a guide for chorionic villi sampling or amniocentesis
■ In second and third trimesters to determine
— Fetal viability/gestational age
— Amniotic fluid volume
— Placental location (also placental anomalies or disorders)
— Uterine and/or fetal anomalies
— As a guide for amniocentesis

Chorionic Villi Sampling (CVS) and Amniocentesis

	CVS	AMNIOCENTESIS
Timing	8 to 12 weeks gestation	14 to 16 weeks' gestation and beyond
Results	1 week	10 days to 2 weeks for genetics; within a few hours for lung maturity and bilirubin
Purposes	Genetic diagnosis	Genetic diagnosis Isoimmunization from Rh disease Lung maturity (L/S) ratio and phosphatidylglycerol (PG)

Review Nursing Care in a nursing textbook or NCLEX Review Manual:
■ *Evolve Reach Comprehensive Review for the NCLEX-RN Examination* (powered by HESI)
■ *Mosby's Comprehensive Review of Nursing for NCLEX-RN Examination*
■ *Saunders Comprehensive Review for the NCLEX-RN Examination*

The nurse is monitoring a client in the first stage of labor and identifies fetal heart rate (FHR) decelerations at the onset of each contraction and a return to the baseline after the contraction. What action should the nurse implement?

A. Discontinue the oxytocin infusion
B. Continue to monitor the FHR
C. Give a bolus of 750 mL D₅LR
D. Insert a fetal scalp electrode

1. Is the item written in a positive or a negative style?

2. Find the key words in the question.

3. Rephrase the question in your own words.

4. Rule out options:
   ■
   ■
   ■

Maternal/Fetal Monitoring

■ Time contractions
— Frequency: from the beginning of one contraction to the beginning of the next contraction
— Duration: length from the beginning to the end
— Intensity: internal monitoring from 30 (mild) to 70 mm Hg (strong)
— Resting tone/time: tension of uterine muscle between contractions and time between contractions
■ Parameters of heart rates
— Normal rate: 110-160 bpm
— Tachycardia: >160 bpm
— Bradycardia: <110 bpm
■ Nursing actions based on fetal heart rate—treat based on cause
■ Reassuring patterns
— Accelerations
■ Non-reassuring patterns:
— Late decelerations (always non-reassuring, even if not very "deep")

Fetal Testing
Nonstress test (NST)

■ Purpose
— Determine fetal well-being
■ Procedure
— External fetal monitor, have mom push marker button with each fetal movement
■ Look for
— Reactivity: a healthy fetus will respond to its own movements by increasing heart rate at least 15 beats for at least 15 seconds; look for two accelerations in 10 minutes or three accelerations in 20 minutes

Contraction Stress Test (CST)/Oxytocin Challenge Test (OCT)

- Purpose
  - — Evaluate the fetus response to stress (contractions)
- Procedure
  - — After obtaining a baseline strip, stimulate contractions by either intravenous oxytocin (Pitocin) or nipple stimulation
- Look for
  - — A negative result in CST
  - — Once three contractions are present in a 10-minute period, should see no late decelerations

Biophysical Profile (BPP)

- Assessment of the physical and physiological characteristics of the developing fetus
- Cataloging of normal and abnormal biophysical responses to stimuli
- The BPP may therefore be considered a physical examination of the fetus
- Exam uses real-time ultrasonography and the NST
- Scoring
  - — 0 or 2 points for each of the five parameters (2 if normal response, 0 if not)
  - — Higher scores indicate healthier fetal status; care provider will use results to develop plan of care
  - — Uses five variables to assess fetal well-being:
    - Fetal breathing movements
    - Gross body movements
    - Fetal tone (flexion)
    - Amniotic fluid volume
    - Reactive (or not) NST

INTRAPARTUM NURSING CARE

A woman who is in labor becomes nauseated, starts hiccupping, and tells her partner to leave her alone. The partner asks the nurse what he did to make this happen. How should the nurse respond?

A. "In active labor, it is quite common for women to react this way. It's nothing you did."

B. "I don't know what you did, but stop because she is quite sensitive right now."

C. "I'll come and examine her. This reaction is common during the transition phase of labor."

D. "Early labor can be very frustrating. I'm sure she doesn't mean to take it out on you."

1. Is the item written in a positive or a negative style?

2. Find the key words in the question.

3. Rephrase the question in your own words.

4. Rule out options:
   -
   -
   -

Differentiation Between True and False Labor

True labor
- Pain in lower back radiating to abdomen
- Regular, rhythmic contractions
- Increased intensity with ambulation
- Progressive cervical dilation and effacement

False Labor
- Discomfort localized to abdomen
- No lower back pain
- Contractions decrease in intensity and/or frequency with ambulation

Vaginal Exam
- Cervical dilation: stretching of cervical os from fingertip diameter to large enough to allow passage of infant (10 cm)
- Effacement: thinning and shortening of the cervix (0% to 100%)
- Station: location of the presenting part in relationship to the mid-pelvis or ischial spines, measured in centimeters above and below.
  — Station 0 = engaged
  — Station +2 = 2 cm below the level of the ischial spines
- Fetal presentation: part of the fetus that presents to the inlet
- Position: relationship of the point of reference (occiput sacrum, acromion) on the fetal presenting part to the mother's pelvis
  — LOA (left occiput anterior)—most common
- Lie: relationship of the long axis (spine) of the fetus to the long axis (spine) of the mother
  — Longitudinal: up and down
  — Transverse: perpendicular
  — Oblique: slanted
- Attitude: relationship of fetal parts to one another
  — Flexion: desired, so that smallest diameters are presented
  — Extension
- Leopold's maneuvers: abdominal palpations used to determine fetal presentation, lie, position, and engagement
- Assessment timing during labor (varies by stage, phase)
- Client responses and nursing interventions for each phase of the first stage of labor vary by phase

The nurse performs a vaginal exam for a laboring client and determines the cervix is dilated 4 cm with 60% effacement, and the presenting part is at −2 station. Thirty minutes later, the client calls and says, "I think my water just broke." Which action has the highest priority?

A. Call the results to the healthcare provider
B. Evaluate the fetal heart rate
C. Help the client to the bathroom for hygiene
D. Perform the Nitrazine and fern tests

1. Is the item written in a positive or a negative style?

2. Find the key words in the question.

3. Rephrase the question in your own words.

4. Rule out options:
   ■
   ■
   ■

Nursing Care During the Second Stage of Labor

■ BP and pulse every 5 to 15 minutes between contractions
■ FHR with each contraction
■ Observe perineal area
  — Bloody show
  — Bulging
  — Visible presenting part
■ Help mother with positions and breathing

Nursing Responsibilities in the Third Stage of Labor

■ Signs of placental separation
  — Lengthening of umbilical cord
  — Gush of blood
  — Uterus changes from discoid to globular
■ Give oxytocin after placenta delivered as prescribed
■ Observe blood loss
■ Ask physician for EBL and time of birth

Nursing Assessment and Interventions in the Fourth Stage of Labor

■ BP, pulse, respirations every 5 minutes for 1 hour, then every 30 minutes until stable
■ Assess fundal firmness and height, bladder, lochia, and perineum every 15 minutes for 1 hour, then every 30 minutes for 2 hours
■ Episiotomy
  — Ice first to minimize edema and anesthetize area (first 24 hours)
  — Then heat to promote healing

Nursing Measures That Promote Bonding/Attachment

■ Encourage initiation of breastfeeding
■ Allow extended time with newborn
■ Withhold eye prophylaxis for up to 2 hours if requested

Nursing Interventions with the Newborn Immediately After Birth

■ Dry infant under warmer or skin to skin with mother
■ Suction mouth and nose

- Assess airway status (retractions, rate, color, expiratory grunt, and nasal flaring)
- Place in "sniff" position
- Determine APGAR score based on heart rate, respiratory effort, muscle tone, reflex irritability, and color: 0 to 2 for each category
- Quick gestational age parameters (preterm vs. term):
  — Sole creases
  — Breast tissue
  — Skin/vessels/creases
  — Genitalia
  — Resting posture

Administration of Analgesic Medication
Drugs used during labor
- Meperidine HCl (Demerol, Pethidine)
- Fentanyl (Sublimaze)
- Morphine sulphate (MS Contin)
- Butorphanol tartrate (Stadol)
- Nalbuphine (Nubain)

Nursing Care Related to Medication
- Withhold if respirations less than 12/min
- Have NARCAN (narcotic antagonist) available
- Monitor respirations, pulse, and BP closely
- Give IV (preferred) or IM
- Obtain drug history

Types of Regional Blocks
- Pudendal block
  — Given in second stage
  — Has no effect on pain of uterine contractions
- Peridural (epidural or caudal) block
  — Given in first or second stage
  — Single dose or continuously
  — May prolong second stage
- Intradural (subarachnoid, spinal)
  — Given second stage
  — Rapid onset
  — Remain flat for 6 to 8 hours after delivery

Assessment and Intervention Before and After Analgesia/Anesthesia
- Assessment before
  — VS and FHR
  — Labor progress
  — Time of last fluid/food ingestion and hydration status
  — Lab values
  — S/S of infection
- Intervention before
  — Prehydrate client
  — Place client in modified Sims position or sitting on side of bed with head flexed

HESI Hint

Review indications, adverse effects and nursing interventions for common intrapartum drugs such as
- Oxytocin
- Methergine
- Demerol
- Stadol
- Nubain
- Morphine and derivatives used in regional anesthesia
- Fentanyl

- Assessment after
  - Ask client to describe symptoms after test dose
  - Assess pain relief
  - BP every 1 to 2 minutes for 15 minutes, then BP every 15 minutes for duration
- Intervention after
  - Assist client to keep bladder empty
  - Assist client with pushing

Care of the Client Receiving General Anesthesia

- Administer drugs to reduce gastric secretions as prescribed
  - Cimetidine (Tagamet) to reduce gastric acid production
  - Sodium citrate (Bicitra) to neutralize gastric acid
- Assist with speedy delivery
- Assess closely for uterine atony by checking fundal firmness and uterine contractions

NORMAL PUERPERIUM (POSTPARTUM)

Normal Anatomical and Physiological Changes

- Cervix
  - Heals within 6 weeks
  - Becomes parous with a transverse slit
- Vagina
  - Rugae within 3 weeks
  - Walls thin and dry
- Breasts (nonlactating)
  - Engorgement 2 to 3 days
- Gastrointestinal
  - Analgesia/anesthesia may decrease peristalsis
  - May have no bowel movement for 2 to 3 days
- Renal
  - Diuresis (up to 3000 mL/day)
  - Bladder distention, urine glucose
  - Creatinine and BUN normal after 7 days
- Cardiac
  - Maternal vascular bed reduces by 15%
  - Pulse may go to 50 bpm
  - Shivering
  - HCT rises
  - Diaphoresis

Normal Postpartal Vital Signs

- Temperature may increase to 100.4° F
- Pulse may decrease to 50 bpm (normal puerperal bradycardia)
- BP should be normal
- Respirations rarely change

Fundal Involution

- Immediately the fundus is several cm below the umbilicus
- Within 12 hours rises to the umbilicus

- Descends 1 cm (fingerbreadth) a day for 9 to 10 days, then fundus is below the symphysis pubis
- Should be midline and firm.

Teaching Points
Perineal care
- Change pads as needed and with voiding/defecation
- Wipe front to back
- Good hand-washing technique
- Ice packs, sitz baths, peri bottle lavage, and topical anesthetic spray and pads

Breastfeeding Advantages
- Milk production
- Let-down reflex
- Breast size
- Diet
- What to avoid
- Care of breasts and nipples
- Engorgement
- Positioning of infant
- Encouragement

Assessment for Thromboembolism
- Pain
- Warmth
- Tenderness
- Swollen vein (tender to touch)
- Intervention to reduce incidence
  - Early ambulation
  - Free movement is encouraged once anesthesia wears off unless an analgesic has been administered.
  - After the initial recovery period is over, the mother is encouraged to ambulate frequently.

Assessment for Maternal Psychological Adaptation and Parent Bonding with the Infant
- Eye contact between mother and infant
- Exploration of infant from head to toe
- Stroking, kissing, and fondling infant
- Smiling, talking, singing to infant
- Absence of negative statements
- Naming newborn quickly

Discharge Teaching
Self-care
- Continue perineal care and pad changes
- Balances diet and fluid intake
- Rest/nap when baby sleeps

Contraceptive Methods
- Sponge with spermicide
- Spermicide alone
- Oral contraceptives
- Transdermal patch

- Vaginal contraceptive ring
- Postcoital contraceptives
- Implant
- IUD (intrauterine device)
- Periodic abstinence
- Surgical sterilization (female or male)

Nursing Implications

Rh$_o$(D) Immune Globulin (RhoGAM)

- Given to Rh-negative women with possible exposure to Rh-positive blood
- Should have negative indirect Coombs' test
- Given IM within 72 hours after delivery
- Checked by two nurses (blood product)

Rubella Vaccine

- Given subcutaneously to nonimmune client before discharge from hospital
- May breastfeed
- Don't give if client or family member is immunocompromised
- Avoid pregnancy for 2 to 3 months (teach contraception)

A client who is 72 hours post cesarean section is preparing to go home. She shares that she cannot get the baby's diaper on "right." Which action should the nurse implement?
A. Demonstrate how to correctly diaper the baby
B. Observe the client diapering the baby while offering praise and hints
C. Call the social worker for long-term follow-up
D. Reassure the client that she knows how to take care of her baby

1. Is the item written in a positive or a negative style?

2. Find the key words in the question.

3. Rephrase the question in your own words.

4. Rule out options:
   -
   -
   -

THE NORMAL NEWBORN

Four births will occur at once. Which birth should the nursery charge nurse assign a newly licensed nurse as her first solo birth and admission?
A. G1 P0 at 39 weeks who will give birth vaginally after a 15-hour induced labor. The mother has been on magnesium sulfate for preeclampsia throughout the labor.
B. G5 P4 at 38 weeks who will give birth vaginally after a 5-hour unmedicated labor. Mild to moderate variable decelerations have been occurring for the last 15 minutes.
C. G3 P1 at 34 weeks who will give birth by cesarean section for a nonreassuring fetal heart rate pattern. The client has a history of cocaine use and has symptoms of abruptio placentae.
D. G2 P1 at 42 weeks who will give birth vaginally after induced labor. The client has been pushing for 2 hours and forceps will be used.

1. Is the item written in a positive or a negative style?

2. Find the key words in the question.

3. Rephrase the question in your own words.

4. Rule out options:
   -
   -
   -

Newborn Vital Sign Parameters and Nursing Implications

- Vital signs
  - T: 97.7° to 99.4° F (may be rectal first, then axillary)
  - P: 110 to 160 bpm (count 1 full minute)
  - R: 110 to 160 breaths/min (count 1 full minute)
- The five signs of respiratory distress in the newborn
  - Tachypnea
  - Cyanosis
  - Nasal flaring
  - Expiratory grunt
  - Retractions

Newborn Parameters

- Caput succedaneum—edema under the scalp, crosses the suture lines
- Cephalhematoma—blood under the periosteum, does not cross suture line
- Fontanel closure
  - Anterior: by 18 months
  - Posterior: 6 to 8 weeks
- Reflexes exhibited by the newborn and age reflexes disappear
  - Rooting: 3 to 4 months
  - Moro: 3 to 4 months
  - Tonic neck: 3 to 4 months
  - Babinski's: 1 year to 18 months
  - Plantar: 8 months
  - Stepping: 3 to 4 months

Nursing Actions for Prevention and/or Treatment

- Aspiration
  - Suction mouth then nose (bulb syringe)
  - Turn on side then pat firmly on back with head 10 to 15 degrees lower than feet
- Infection
  - HAND WASHING
  - Effective cord care
  - Encourage breastfeeding
- Hypothermia
  - Keep warm and dry
  - Stockinette cap
  - Assess temperature every 4 to 6 hours
- Hypoglycemia
  - Keep warm
  - Heel stick on sides of heel
- Diabetes mellitus type 1
  - Jittery babies or babies with high-pitched cry
  - Feed if glucose level <40 mg/dL
- Hemorrhagic disorders
  - Administer vitamin K
- Hyperbilirubinemia
  - Evaluate Rh isoimmunization
  - Monitor bilirubin
  - Keep hydrated
  - Promote feeding and stooling
  - Monitor for jaundice

Review Newborn Physical Exam in a textbook or NCLEX Review Manual:

- *Evolve Reach Comprehensive Review for the NCLEX-RN Examination* (powered by HESI)
- *Mosby's Comprehensive Review of Nursing for NCLEX-RN Examination*
- *Saunders Comprehensive Review for the NCLEX-RN Examination*

119

Jaundice Differentiation

- Physiological jaundice: after 24 hours
- Pathological jaundice: before 24 hours, persist >7 days

The Procedure for Performing a Heel Stick

- Avoid plantar artery
- Only lateral surfaces of heel
- Use a heel warmer

Vitamin K

- Give vitamin K in the vastus lateralis to prevent hemorrhagic disorder in newborn

Newborn Respirations

- It is not safe to nipple feed a newborn if the respiration rate exceeds 60 breaths/min

Newborn Teaching Points

- Feeding
- Bathing
- Diapering
- Crying patterns
- Comfort measures for fussy babies
- Signs and symptoms of illness in a newborn that warrant a call to the healthcare provider

ANTEPARTUM/ INTRAPARTUM HIGH-RISK DISORDERS

Chronic Hypertensive Disorders

A 33-week-gestational woman who is diagnosed with pregnancy-induced hypertension (PIH) is admitted to the labor and delivery area. She is obviously nervous and expresses concern for the health of her baby. How should the nurse respond?
A. "You have the best doctor on the staff, so don't worry about a thing."
B. "Your anxiety is contributing to your condition and may be the reason for your admission."
C. "This is a minor problem that is easily controlled, and everything will be all right."
D. "As I assess you and your baby, I will explain the plan for your care and answer your questions."

Chronic Hypertension

- Hypertension and/or proteinuria in pregnant woman with chronic hypertension prior to 20 weeks of gestation and persistent after 12 weeks post partum

Superimposed Preeclampsia or Eclampsia

- Development of preeclampsia or eclampsia in woman with chronic hypertension prior to 20 weeks of gestation

Preeclampsia/Eclampsia

- Pathophysiology
  — Think about what decreased perfusion does to all the organs

1. Is the item written in a positive or a negative style?

2. Find the key words in the question.

3. Rephrase the question in your own words.

4. Rule out options:
   -
   -
   -

HESI Hint

Magnesium sulfate is *not* an antihypertensive; it is used to prevent/control seizure. Withhold if any of the following is present:
- R <12 breaths/min
- Absent deep tendon reflexes (DTRs)
- Urine output <30 mL/hr

- HELLP syndrome—extremely severe form of gestational hypertension:
  Hemolysis, **E**levated **L**iver Enzymes, **L**ow **P**latelets

- Preeclampsia symptoms
  — BP
    - Mild: 30 mm Hg systolic and/or 15 mm Hg diastolic over baseline
    - Severe: Same (some sources say 160/110 mm Hg × 2 or more)
  — Protein
    - Mild: >1+
    - Severe: 3+ to 4+
  — Edema
    - Mild: Eyes, face, fingers
    - Severe: Generalized edema
  — Deep tendon reflexes (DTRs)
    - Mild: 3+
    - Severe: 3+ or more and clonus
  — Central nervous system (CNS) symptoms
    - Mild: Headache, irritability
    - Severe: Severe headache, visual disturbances
  — Other
    - Weight gain >2 lb/week
    - Oliguria (<100 mL/4 hr); epigastric pain related to liver enlargement
    - Elevated serum creatinine, thrombocytopenia, marked SGOT elevation
- Nursing Interventions: Preeclampsia
  — Control stimulation in room
  — Explain procedures
  — Maintain IV (16 to 18 g venocatheter)
  — Monitor BP q 15 to 30 min and DTRs and urine for protein q 1 hr
  — Administer magnesium sulfate as prescribed
  — Monitor magnesium levels and signs of toxicity (urinary output <30 mL/hr, R <12, DTRs absent, deceleration of FHR, bradycardia)
- Nursing Interventions: Eclampsia
  What to do if client seizes:
  — Stay with client
  — Turn client to side
  — Do not attempt to force objects into client's mouth
  — Administer O$_2$ and have suction available
  — Give magnesium sulfate as prescribed

HESI Hint

Remember that seizures can occur postpartum.

Gestational Diabetes

- Predisposing factors
  — Family history of diabetes
  — History of more than two spontaneous abortions
  — Hydramnios
  — Previous baby with weight > 4000 g (8 lb 13.5 oz)
  — Previous baby with congenital anomalies

— High parity
— Obesity
— Recurrent monilial vaginitis
— Glycosuria
— Abnormal glucose screen

Screening

■ Recommendations for glucose screening for all pregnant women
— 1-hour glucose screen between 24 and 26 weeks

Changing Insulin Needs during Pregnancy

■ Decrease in first trimester
■ Increase in second and third trimesters
■ Back to prepregnancy schedule post partum unless breastfeeding, which keeps need for insulin lower

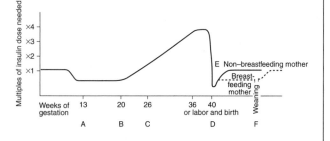

■ **Infants of diabetic mothers are at risk for:**
— Clavicular fractures
— Cerebral trauma
— Prematurity
— Hypoglycemia
— Hypocalcemia
— Hyperbilirubinemia
— Polycythemia
— Infection
— Macrosomia or intrauterine growth retardation (IUGR)
— Congenital anomalies

A client who has gestational diabetes asks the nurse to explain the reason why her baby is at risk for macrosomia. Which explanation should the nurse offer?
A. The placenta receives decreased maternal blood flow during pregnancy because of vascular constriction.
B. The fetus secretes insulin in response to maternal hyperglycemia, causing weight gain and growth.
C. Infants of diabetic mothers are postmature which allows the fetus extra time to grow.
D. Rapid fetal growth contributes to congenital anomalies, which are more common in infants of diabetic mothers.

HESI Hint

Insulin
■ Generally, oral hypoglycemics are not used in pregnancy because they cross the placenta. Insulin is used because it does not cross the placenta.
■ *Only* *regular* insulin is used during labor because it is short acting, which makes it easier to maintain the mother's glucose level at 60 to 100 mg/dL.

1. **Is the item written in a positive or a negative style?**

2. **Find the key words in the question.**

3. **Rephrase the question in your own words.**

4. **Rule out options:**
   ■
   ■
   ■

Preterm Labor (PTL)

- Signs of PTL
  - More than five contractions in an hour (painful or painless)
  - Menstrual-like cramps
  - Low, dull backache
  - Pelvic pressure
  - Increase/change in vaginal discharge
  - Leaking or gush of amniotic fluid

Teaching Points for Home Management of PTL

- Bed rest (fetus off the cervix)
- May be on home monitoring
- Side-lying and elevate foot of bed to increase uterine perfusion
- Side effects and warning signs of tocolytic drugs
- Avoid sexual stimulation
- Increase oral fluid (2 to 3 L/day)
- Empty bladder q 2 hr
- Review what to do if membranes rupture or if signs of infection occur.

Tocolytics and Their Administration

The medications used for cessation of uterine contractions include:

- Ritodrine (Yutopar)
  - Side effects
    - Nervousness
    - Tremulousness
    - Headache
    - N/V, diarrhea
    - Epigastric pain
  - Adverse effects
    - Tachycardia
    - Chest pain
    - Pulmonary edema
    - Low K$^+$
    - Hyperglycemia
  - Nursing interventions
    - Maternal ECG and lab tests
    - Bedside cardiac monitor
    - Monitor fetus
    - VS q 15 min
  - Antidotes
    - Propranolol (Inderal)
    - Beta blocker
- Terbutaline (Brethine)
  - Side effects
    - Nervousness
    - Tremulousness
    - Headache
    - N/V, diarrhea
    - Epigastric pain

HESI Hint

Betamethasone (Celestone) is used in PTL to enhance surfactant production and fetal lung maturity if fetus is <35 weeks of gestation.

HESI Hint

Review what to do if membranes rupture or if signs of infection occur
Infection symptoms:

- Chills
- T >100.4° F
- Dysuria
- Pain in abdomen
- Fluid discharge from vagina
- Change in fetal movement and/or increased FHR

- — Adverse effects
  - Tachycardia
  - Chest pain
  - Pulmonary edema
  - Low K$^+$
  - Hyperglycemia
  - — Nursing interventions
  - Maternal pulse not >140 bpm
  - FHR not >180 bpm
  - Monitor I & O
  - Check weight daily
  - — Antidotes
  - Propranolol (Inderal)
  - Beta blocker
- ■ Magnesium sulfate
  - — Side effects
    - CNS depression
    - Slowed respirations
    - Decreased DTRs
  - — Adverse effects
    - Decreased urine output
    - Pulmonary edema
  - — Nursing interventions
    - Hold if R <12/min
    - Urine output < 100 mL/4 hr
    - Absent DTRs
    - Monitor serum magnesium levels
  - — Antidote
    - Calcium gluconate
- ■ Additional drugs used to decrease contractions
  - — Indomethacin (Indocin)
  - — Nifedipine (Procardia)

Hemorrhagic Disorders

- ■ Spontaneous abortion (miscarriage)
- ■ Incompetent cervix
- ■ Molar pregnancy
- ■ Ectopic pregnancy
- ■ Abruptio placentae
- ■ Placenta previa
- ■ DIC (disseminated intravascular coagulation)

A client at 15 weeks of gestation is admitted for an inevitable abortion. Thirty minutes after returning from surgery, her vital signs are stable. Which intervention has the highest priority?

A. Ask the client if she would like to talk about losing her baby.

B. Place cold cabbage leaves on the client's breasts to decrease breast engorgement.

C. Send a referral to the grief counselor for at-home follow-up

D. Confirm the client's Rh and Coombs' status and administer RhoGAM if indicated.

1. **Is the item written in a positive or a negative style?**

2. **Find the key words in the question.**

3. **Rephrase the question in your own words.**

4. **Rule out options:**
   - ■
   - ■
   - ■

Miscarriage

- Assessment
  - Vaginal bleeding with a gestational age of 20 weeks or less
  - Uterine cramping, backache, and pelvic pressure
  - Maybe symptoms of shock
  - Assess client/family emotional status, needs, and support
- Interventions
  - ID type of abortion: threatened, inevitable, complete, septic, missed, or recurrent
  - Monitor VS, LOC, and amount of bleeding
  - IV 18 gauge over-the-needle catheter
  - Implement grief protocol
  - If client Rh negative, give RhoGAM

Incompetent Cervix

- Incompetent cervix (recurrent premature dilation of the cervix) is defined as passive and painless dilation of the cervix during the second trimester.
- Risk factors
  - Prior traumatic delivery
  - History of dilatation and curettage (D&C)
  - Multiple abortions (spontaneous or induced)
- Conservative management
  - Bed rest
  - Hydration
  - Tocolysis (inhibition of uterine contractions)
- A cervical cerclage may be performed.
  - McDonald cerclage: a band of homologous fascia or nonabsorbable ribbon (Mersilene) may be placed around the cervix beneath the mucosa to constrict the internal os of the cervix.
  - A cerclage procedure can be classified according to time, or whether it is elective (prophylactic), urgent, or emergent.

Ectopic Pregnancy

- Assessment
  - Missed period but early signs of pregnancy absent
  - Positive pregnancy test
  - Rupture
    - Sharp unilateral pelvic pain
    - Vaginal bleeding
    - Referred shoulder pain
    - Syncope can lead to shock
- Interventions
  - STAT VS
  - Check for bleeding
  - IV
  - Prepare client for ultrasound
  - Prepare client for possible laparotomy
  - Preoperative and postoperative care
  - Type and cross-match for two or more units of blood or packed cells

Abruptio Placentae and Placenta Previa

- Abruptio placentae
  - Concealed or overt bleeding
  - Uterine tone ranges from tense without relaxation to tense and boardlike
  - Persistently painful
  - Abnormal fetal heart rate (the more area abrupted, the worse the FHR)
- Placenta previa
  - Bright red vaginal bleeding
  - Soft uterine tone
  - Painless
  - FHR is normal unless bleeding is severe and mother become hypovolemic

Nursing Interventions for Abruptio Placentae

- Monitor BP and pulse q 15 min
- Closely monitor uterine contractions and FHR with an external monitor
- Client in side-lying position
- IV 16 to 18 gauge catheter
- Draw blood for CBC clotting studies, Rh factor, type/cross-match
- Watch for signs of DIC
- Monitor blood loss
- Prepare for emergency cesarean delivery

Nursing Interventions for Placenta Previa

- Bed rest until fetal lungs mature
- Monitor BP and pulse q 15 min
- Start IV
- Draw blood for CBC clotting studies, Rh factor, type/cross-match
- Monitor contractions and FHR with external monitor
- Client in side-lying position
- Monitor blood loss
- Prepare client for ultrasound
- Prepare client/family for possible cesarean birth

Disseminated Intravascular Coagulation

- Risk factors for DIC in pregnancy
  - Fetal demise
  - Infection/sepsis
  - Pregnancy-induced hypertension (preeclampsia)
  - Abruptio placentae

Dystocia

- A difficult birth resulting from problems of the "5 Ps" (powers, passage, passenger, psyche, and/or position); that is, a lack of progress in cervical dilatation, delay in fetal descent, or change in uterine contraction characteristics suggest dystocia.

HESI Hint

If abruption or previa is suspected or confirmed, NO abdominal or vaginal manipulation such as

- Leopold's maneuvers
- Vaginal exams
- Internal monitor (especially if previa)
- Rectal exams/enemas/suppositories

Artificial Rupture of Membranes

- Nursing care during and after artificial rupture of membranes (AROM)
  — Explain procedure (painless)
  — Assess FHR immediately after rupture (prolapsed cord)
  — Assess fluid (color, odor, consistency)

Hyperemesis Gravidarum

- When vomiting during pregnancy becomes excessive enough to cause weight loss of at least 5% of prepregnancy weight and is accompanied by dehydration, electrolyte imbalance, ketosis, and acetonuria

The Client Undergoing Cesarean Delivery
Is at Risk for:

- Paralytic ileus
  — Related to bowel manipulation, decreased activity, and use of some pain medications
- Aspiration pneumonia (especially with general anesthesia)
- Thromboembolism
  — Related to decreased activity postop besides the normal increased risk of this disorder in pregnancy
- Post-birth pain (multiple layers of cut/pulled/sewn tissue)
- Uterine rupture in future pregnancies (especially if vertical uterine incision)
- UTI (because she has a Foley catheter)
- Having a baby with transient tachypnea (TTN)
- No "squeeze" through vagina for baby

Cesarean Birth Nursing Care
Preoperative

- If planned, encourage couple to attend classed
- If emergency, make sure informed consent is signed and on the chart
- Assist with anesthesia
- Administer preoperative medications
- Prepare client for surgery
  — Foley catheter
  — Lab tests
  — Urinalysis
  — Shave(?)
- Safely transport client
- Allow presence of support person

Intraoperative

- Place a wedge under right hip, keep warm, monitor and record FHR
- Apply grounding pad to leg
- Abdominal scrub
- If client awake, assess and meet needs

Postoperative

- Receive complete report
- Note fundal height and tone
- Assess T q 1 hr (recovery) then q 4 hr for 24 hours
- Assess BP, pulse, respirations, breath sounds, bowel sounds, and Sao_2
- Begin I & O q 8 hr
- Administer pain medication as prescribed

POSTPARTUM HIGH-RISK DISORDERS

Postpartum Infections

- Predisposing factors
  - Rupture of membranes > 24 hr
  - Any laceration or operative incision
  - Hemorrhage
  - Hematomas
  - Lapses in aseptic technique before and after delivery
  - Anemia or poor physical health prior to delivery
  - Intrauterine manipulation, manual removal of placenta, retained placental fragments
- Infections
  - Perineal infections
  - Endometritis
  - Parametritis
  - Peritonitis
  - Mastitis
  - Deep vein thrombosis
  - Cystitis
  - Pyelonephritis
  - HIV, hepatitis, other STIs

HESI Hint

Review about various infective agents and the drugs that treat them in a textbook or NCLEX Review Manual

- *Evolve Reach Comprehensive Review for the NCLEX-RN Examination* (powered by HESI)
- *Mosby's Comprehensive Review of Nursing for NCLEX-RN Examination*
- *Saunders Comprehensive Review for the NCLEX-RN Examination*

Rooming-in and Breastfeeding Recommendations		
CONDITION	ROOMING-IN	BREASTFEEDING
HIV/AIDS	Yes	No
Cytomegalovirus (CMV)	Yes	No
Chlamydia	Yes	Yes
Gonorrhea (untreated)	No	No
Medication × 24 hr	Yes	Yes
Hepatitis	Yes	Yes
Herpes	Yes	Yes
Syphilis (untreated)	No	No
Medication × 24 hr	Yes	Yes
Trichomoniasis	Yes	Yes

Postpartum (PP) Hemorrhage

Causes

- Uterine atony
- Lacerations of vagina or cervix
- Cervix, perineum, or labia hematomas
- Retained placental fragments
- Full bladder

Predisposing Factors

- High parity
- Dystocia, prolonged labor
- Operative delivery, forceps delivery
- Interuterine manipulation
- Overdistention of uterus (polyhydramnios, multiple gestation, large fetus)
- Abruptio placentae
- Previous history of postpartum hemorrhage
- Infection
- Placenta previa

Differentiating Causes

- Uterine atony
  - Most common causes are retained placenta, full bladder, prolonged use of Pitocin in labor, overdistention of uterus
  - Signs: uterus is boggy, usually umbilicus, fundus does not firm with massage, >1 pad/hr saturated
    - How to most accurately estimate blood loss when doing a "pad count" (1 g = 1 mL)
  - Minimal, if any, pain
- Hematomas
  - Associated with operative delivery, including forceps; may also occur in labia
  - Signs: swelling and blue-black discoloration; however, if vaginal wall may not be obvious, feeling of pressure in vagina, urethra, or bladder, signs of shock without obvious frank bleeding
  - Intense pain as size increases
- Lacerations
  - Associated with operative delivery, including forceps
  - Signs: may see either continuous trickle or bleeding in spurts, fundus is firm
  - "Normal" pain from postdelivery uterine contractions

Nursing Interventions

- Early PP hemorrhage
  - Monitor VS, fundus, lochia q 1 hr
  - Monitor LOC
  - Keep bladder empty
  - Count pads and times
  - Monitor I & O
  - Call physician if atony/bleeding continue despite massage
  - Anticipate increasing Pitocin or giving ergot

- Late PP hemorrhage
  — Type/cross-match
  — Administer oxytocin or ergot
  — Administer antibiotics as prescribed
  — Keep client warm
  — Be alert for shock
  — Possibly prepare client for surgical repair or removal of placental fragments
- Hematoma
  — Apply ice to perineum
  — Prepare client for surgical evacuation if large
  — Monitor VS
  — Administer analgesics and antibiotics as prescribed
  — Be alert for shock

The nurse receives shift reports on four postpartum clients. Which client should the nurse assess first?
A. G3 P3, 7 hours after forceps delivery, who is complaining of pain and perineal pressure unrelieved by analgesics
B. G1 P1, 8 hours after cesarean delivery who is receiving IV Pitocin and complaining of cramping with increased lochia when sitting
C. G2 P2, 5 hours after vaginal delivery, complaining of abdominal pain when the infant breastfeeds
D. G7 P6, 6 hours after vaginal delivery of twins, who reports saturating one pad in a 3-hour period

1. Is the item written in a positive or a negative style?

2. Find the key words in the question.

3. Rephrase the question in your own words.

4. Rule out options:
   -
   -
   -

NEWBORN HIGH-RISK DISORDERS

Which nursing action has the highest priority for an infant immediately after birth?
A. Place the infant's head in the "sniff" position and give oxygen via face mask
B. Perform a bedside glucose test and feed the infant glucose water as needed
C. Assess the heart rate and perform chest compressions if rate is less than 60 bpm
D. Dry the infant and place under a radiant warmer or skin-to-skin with the mother

1. Is the item written in a positive or a negative style?

2. Find the key words in the question.

3. Rephrase the question in your own words.

4. Rule out options:
   -
   -
   -

Major Danger Signals in the Newborn
Central Nervous System
- Lethargy, high-pitched cry, jitteriness, seizures, bulging fontanels

Respiratory System
- Apnea, tachypnea, flaring nares, retractions, seesaw breathing, grunting, abnormal blood gases

Cardiovascular System
- Abnormal rate and rhythm, persistent murmurs, differentials in pulse, dusky skin color, and circumoral cyanosis

Gastrointestinal System

- Absent feeding reflexes, vomiting, abdominal distention, changes in stool patterns, no stool

Metabolic System

- Hypoglycemia, hypocalcemia, hyperbilirubinemia, labile temperature

Metabolic System Birth Weight Risks

- Low birth weight (LBW), ≤2500 g
- Very low birth weight (VLBW), ≤1500 g

Newborn Resuscitation Guidelines

- Bag and mask ventilations—40 to 60 breaths/min
- Cardiac compressions—120 events per min (90 compression : 30 ventilations)
- Start IV fluids (usually umbilical vein)
- Administer sodium bicarbonate and/or epinephrine and glucose as prescribed
- Assign someone to support parents
- May use Silverman-Anderson Index of Respiratory Distress to evaluate

Signs of Neonatal Sepsis

- Lethargy
- Temperature instability
- Difficulty feeding
- Subtle color changes (mottling, duskiness)
- Subtle changes in behavior ("just acts funny")
- Respiratory distress, apnea
- Hyperbilirubinemia

Prematurity

- Respiratory distress
  — Lung immaturity, lack of surfactant lining alveoli, immaturity of respiratory center in the brain (apnea and bradycardia), PDA, RDS (hypoxia and hypercarbia
- Temperature instability
  — Insufficient subcutaneous fat, larger ratio of body surface to weight, extended position, immature hypothalamus
- Nutritional problems
  — Poor suck, small stomach, immature digestion, hypoglycemia, anemia, hyperbilirubinemia
- Fluid and electrolyte problems
  — Limited concentration/excretion of kidneys, metabolic acidosis, hypocalcemia (7 mg/dL, inability to store/absorb calcium)
- Immunological difficulties
  — No IgM antibodies, no phagocytosis, thin skin, IVH

Hyperbilirubinemia

- Identify predisposing risk factors.
  — Rh or ABO incompatibility
  — Prematurity
  — IUGR Pitocin induction

HESI Hints

- Review nursing interventions to prevent/alleviate problems of prematurity
- Be aware of the importance of developmentally appropriate stimulation: not too little, not too much
  — Failure to thrive
  — Avoidance of eye contact with people
  — Absent weak crying
- How to convert weight from pounds to kilograms for drug calculations:

  Divide lb by 2.2.
  Example: 6 lb ÷ 2.2 = 2.72 kg

131

— Sepsis
— Perinatal asphyxia
— Maternal diabetes mellitus
— Intrauterine infection
— Cephalhematoma

- The preterm infant is more likely to develop jaundice because of liver immaturity.

Jaundice

- Early and frequent feedings are thought to help prevent jaundice (physiological) in infants because bilirubin is excreted via the stools.
  — Breast milk contains a natural laxative, so it works especially well.
- Assessment for jaundice in infants
  — Light-skinned: apply pressure with thumb over bony prominences to blanch skin, remove thumb, and area will appear yellow before normal skin color reappears
  — Dark-skinned: observe conjunctival sac and oral mucosa

Nursing Interventions for Infants Undergoing Phototherapy

- Place unclothed neonate 18 inches below a bank of lights for several hours or days until bilirubin levels <12 mg/dL
- Place opaque mask over eyes to prevent retinal damage
- Monitor skin temperature
- Cover genitals with a small diaper or mask to catch urine/stool while leaving skin surface open to light
- Turn q 2 hr to avoid skin breakdown
- Maintain hydration
- Monitor for dehydration

A pregnant client tells the nurse that she smokes only a few cigarettes a day. What information should the nurse provide the client about the effects of smoking during pregnancy?
A. Smoking causes vasoconstriction and decreases placental perfusion.
B. Smoking decreases the L:S ratio, contributing to lung immaturity.
C. Smoking causes vasodilation and increased fluid overload for the fetus.
D. Smoking during pregnancy places the fetus at risk for lung cancer.

Exposure to Cigarette Smoking While in Utero

Symptoms

- Small neonate
- IUGR
- Neonates of mothers who are exposed to smoke-filled environment are also at risk

1. Is the item written in a positive or a negative style?

2. Find the key words in the question.

3. Rephrase the question in your own words.

4. Rule out options:
   -
   -
   -

Nursing Interventions

- Teach client IUGR can be minimized or eliminated if she stops smoking early in pregnancy
- Treat infant as small-for-gestational-age infant (SGA)

Neonatal Narcotic Withdrawal Syndrome

Symptoms

- Irritability
- Hyperactivity
- High-pitched cry
- Coarse flapping
- Tremors
- Poor feeding
- Frantic sucking
- Vomiting/diarrhea
- Nasal stuffiness

Nursing Interventions

- Swaddle and minimize handling
- Decrease environmental stimuli
- Provide pacifier
- Place in prone position with sheepskin
- Cover elbows, knees to prevent skin breakdown
- Keep bulb syringe close

Fetal Alcohol Syndrome (FAS)

Symptoms

- Microcephaly
- Growth retardation
- Short palpebral fissures
- Maxillary hypoplasia

Nursing Interventions

- Determine how much and how often the mother drank during pregnancy and/or while breastfeeding (most harmful at 16th to 18th weeks)
- Decrease environmental stimuli
- Provide enteral feedings if neonate has uncoordinated sucking and swallowing

Long-Term Complications

- Mental retardation
- Poor coordination
- Facial abnormalities
- Behavioral deviations (irritability)
- Cardiac and joint abnormalities

HESI Hint

The combined effects of cigarette smoking and alcohol consumption during pregnancy causes greater fetal anomalies than the sum of their individual effects.

8 Psychiatric Nursing

THERAPEUTIC COMMUNICATION

Therapeutic communication is the goal-directed exchange of verbal and nonverbal interactions.
- Nonverbal interaction
  — May be more important than verbal communication
- Verbal communications
  — Promote insight and help client to problem solve
  — Must keep client as focus
  — Allow client to make choices
  — JUST FACTS!
  — Use matter-of-fact approach

Communication Techniques
- Acknowledgment:
  — Affirm client without imposing own values
- Clarifying:
  — Making sure you understand client
- Confrontation:
  — Calling attention to inconsistent behavior
- Focusing:
  — Assisting client to explore topic
- Information-giving:
  — Feedback about client's behavior
- Open-ended:
  — Questions require more than "yes" or "no" answer
- Reflecting/restating:
  — Paraphrasing/repeating what the client said
- Silence:
  — Therapeutic or used to control interaction
- Suggesting:
  — Offering alternatives

Practice these phrases:
- "Tell me about …"
- "Go on …"
- "What are your thoughts?"
- "What are you feeling?"
- "It seems as if …"
- "Are you saying that …"

Avoid these phrases:
- "You should …"
- "You can't …"
- "Let's …"
- "Why don't you …"
- "I think you …"
- "Everyone …"
- "Why …?"
- "I know …"

HESI Hint

When a client discloses information to the nurse and then asks the nurse to avoid telling anyone …

The best response is to explain to the client that "information that is relevant to your treatment plan must be shared with the treatment team," especially if the client has thoughts of harm to self or others.

A female client who just learned that she has breast cancer told her family that the biopsy was negative. What action should the nurse take?

A. Remind the client that the results were positive
B. Ask the client to restate what the healthcare provider told her
C. Talk to the family about the client's need for family support
D. Encourage the client to talk to the nurse about her fears

Some Common Coping Styles (Defense Mechanisms)

- Denial
- Identification
- Intellectualization
- Projection
- Rationalization
- Repression
- Regression
- Suppression
- Displacement

THERAPEUTIC TREATMENT MODALITIES

- Milieu therapy
- Behavior modification
- Family therapy
- Crisis intervention
- Cognitive therapy
- Electroconvulsive therapy (ECT)

The nurse is facilitating a support group about stress management. During the initial phase, a female group member states that she can help the group more because she has a master's degree. How should the nurse respond?

A. Restate the purpose of the support group sessions
B. Ask the group to identify various stressful problems
C. Obtain ideas from the members about strategies for stressful situations
D. Conclude the meeting and evaluate the session

1. Is the item written in a positive or a negative style?

2. Find the key words in the question.

3. Rephrase the question in your own words.

4. Rule out options:
   -
   -
   -

1. Is the item written in a positive or a negative style?

2. Find the key words in the question.

3. Rephrase the question in your own words.

4. Rule out options:
   -
   -
   -

Group Interventions
- May be closed or open groups
- May be small or large (>10)
- Multiple types of groups:
  — Psychoeducation
  — Supportive therapy
  — Psychotherapy
  — Self-help
- Common nurse-led groups:
  — Medication
  — Symptom management
  — Anger management
  — Self-care

Group Work Phases
- Members in the *initial phase* will have
  — High anxiety
  — Superficial interactions
  — Questions about trusting the therapist
- Members in the *middle/working phase* will
  — Identify problems
  — Begin problem solving
  — Develop sense of "we-ness"
- Members in the *termination phase*
  — Evaluate the experience
  — May experience emotions from anger to joy

The nurse takes a group of mental health clients to a baseball game. During the game, a male client begins to complain of shortness of breath and dizziness. Which intervention should the nurse implement first?
A. Send the client back to the unit
B. Ask for a description of his feelings
C. Escort the client to a quiet area
D. Inquire about what is most stressful

ANXIETY AND RELATED DISORDERS

Levels of Anxiety
- Mild
  — Occurs daily
  — Motivates learning
  — Adequate concentration
  — Calm/in control
- Moderate
  — Motivates learning
  — Adequate concentration
  — Restless
  — Some physical symptoms
  — Dull sensory perceptions

1. Is the item written in a positive or a negative style?

2. Find the key words in the question.

3. Rephrase the question in your own words.

4. Rule out options:
   -
   -
   -

- Severe
  - "Fight or flight" response
  - Selective attention
  - Sensory stimuli disorganized
- Panic
  - Immediate intervention needed
  - Feels overwhelmed, helpless
  - Unable to concentrate

GENERALIZED ANXIETY

Nursing Diagnoses
- Anxiety
- Ineffective Coping
- Impaired Social Interaction
- Posttraumatic Stress Response

Nursing Assessment
- Severe anxiety/tension
- Autonomic hyperactivity
- Sleep disturbance
- Difficulty concentrating
- Irritability

Nursing Interventions
- Help client identify relationship between stressor and level of anxiety
- Assist client in trying different coping behaviors
- Encourage exercise, deep breathing, relaxation, and visualization
- Decrease environmental stimuli

Panic Disorder and Phobias
- Irrational *fear* of an object, activity, or situation
- Anxiety is transferred from its source to an object or situation
- Client is aware of excessive fear, but "can't help it"
- A chronic condition that has exacerbations and remissions

Common Coping Mechanisms
- Displacement
- Projection
- Repression
- Sublimation

Nursing Interventions
- Establish trust and safety
- Refocus attention
- Educate about alternative coping strategies
- Desensitize client, gradually introduce stimuli
- Discuss fears/feelings
- Give SSRIs and other medications as needed
- Decrease caffeine and nicotine

The nurse is planning to teach a male client strategies for coping with his anxiety. The nurse finds him in his room compulsively washing his hands. What action should the nurse take next?
A. Teach alternatives as he washes his hands
B. Ask him to stop his hand washing immediately
C. Allow him to finish hand washing before teaching
D. Ask what precipitated the hand washing

Obsessive-Compulsive Disorder
- Obsessions:
    — Repetitive thoughts
- Compulsions:
    — Impulses to perform action
    — *The client experiences feelings of losing control*

Nursing Diagnoses
- Impaired Social Interaction
- Ineffective Individual Coping

Common Coping Mechanisms
- Repression
- Isolation
- Undoing

Further Assessment
- Destructive, hostile, aggressive, and delusional thoughts related to the compulsive action
- Difficulty with relationships and interference with daily activities

Nursing Interventions
- Address physical needs
- Avoid criticism of behavior
- Establish routine to avoid anxiety-producing changes
- Assist client to learn alternative methods to cope
- Give SSRIs, tricyclic antidepressants, or other medications as needed
- Allow client to perform compulsive activity, then limit the amount of time and encourage client to gradually decrease the time

Post-Traumatic Stress Disorder
Severe anxiety that results from a traumatic experience

Nursing Diagnosis
- Posttraumatic Syndrome
- Ineffective Individual Coping

Assessment
- Symptomatic behaviors
    — Intrusive thoughts, flashbacks
    — Nightmares, emotional detachment

1. **Is the item written in a positive or a negative style?**

2. **Find the key words in the question.**

3. **Rephrase the question in your own words.**

4. **Rule out options:**
    -
    -
    -

Common Responses

- Shock
- Anger
- Panic
- Denial

Nursing Interventions

- Implement safety precautions if needed
- Assist client to identify past situations handled successfully
- Give antianxiety and antipsychotic medications

Frequently Used Medications

- Selective serotonin reuptake inhibitors (SSRIs)
  — Fluvoxamine (Luvox)
  — Fluoxetine (Prozac)
  — Paroxetine (Paxil)
  — Sertraline (Zoloft)
- Tricyclic antidepressants
  — Amitriptyline (Elavil)
  — Imipramine (Tofranil)
- Benzodiazepines
  — Alprazolam (Xanax)
  — Chlordiazepoxide (Librium)
  — Clonazepam (Klonopin)
  — Diazepam (Valium)
  — Lorazepam (Ativan)
- Nonbenzodiazepines
  — Buspirone (BuSpar)
  — Zolpidem (Ambien)

Somatoform Disorders

- Include a group of disorders that convert anxiety into physical symptoms for which there is no identifiable physical diagnosis.
- Reflect complex interactions between the mind and the body with serious impairment in the person's social and occupational functioning.
- Formerly called hysteria and Briquet's syndrome.

Types of Somatization Disorder

- Conversion disorder
- Pain disorder
- Hypochondriasis
- Body dysmorphic disorder

Common Defenses

- Conversion
- Displacement
- Projection
- Somatization
- Denial

Note: Remember that defenses protect the client from anxiety.

Nursing Diagnoses

- Alteration in Comfort, Chronic Pain
- Ineffective Coping

Review the side effects, adverse effects, actions, and nursing implications of these medications in a nursing textbook or an NCLEX Review Manual:

- *Evolve Reach Comprehensive Review for the NCLEX-RN Examination* (powered by HESI)
- *Mosby's Comprehensive Review of Nursing for NCLEX-RN Examination*
- *Saunders Comprehensive Review for the NCLEX-RN Examination*

HESI Hint

For these drugs it is important to know

- Which drugs are in what categories
- Indications for use
- Adverse reactions
- Drug-drug interactions
- Nursing implications

While the nurse is talking to a client who has a dissociative identity disorder, the client begins to dissociate during the interaction. Which action should the nurse implement?
A. Escort the client to art therapy group
B. Call the client by name
C. Talk about stressful feelings
D. Move to another setting

Dissociative Disorders

Dissociative Amnesia

- Defining symptom is one or more episodes of inability to recall important personal information, usually of a traumatic or stressful nature, that is too extensive to be attributed to ordinary forgetting.

Dissociative Fugue

- Dissociative fugue is a sudden, unexpected travel away from home or one's customary place of work, with an inability to recall one's past (or where one has been).

Dissociative Identity Disorder

- The first criterion is that the individual must demonstrate two or more distinct identities or personality states.
- The second criterion is that at least two of these personality states recurrently take control of the person's behavior.

Depersonalization Disorder

- Persistent or recurrent episodes of feelings of detachment or estrangement from one's self. Sensations of being outside of one's body or mental processes or being an observer of one's body often occur.

Personality Disorders

- Remember the 3 Ps:
  — *Pervasive, persistent,* and *patterns of behavior*

Cluster A (Odd and Eccentric)

- Paranoid
- Schizoid
- Schizotypal

Cluster B (Emotional and Dramatic)

- Antisocial
- Borderline
- Histrionic
- Narcissistic

Cluster C (Anxious and Tense)

- Avoidant
- Dependent
- Obsessive-compulsive

Note: Manipulation and power struggle are common in relationships of a person with a personality disorder.

1. Is the item written in a positive or a negative style?

2. Find the key words in the question.

3. Rephrase the question in your own words.

4. Rule out options:
   -
   -
   -

Personality Disorders and Manipulation

- Identify manipulative behaviors
- Assist client to recognize manipulative behaviors
- Set clear, *consistent* limits; follow through with consequences
- Communicate expectations clearly with client and staff
- Focus on strengths and effective communication skills
- Encourage socialization with others to improve skills
- Protect client from harm to self or others, as needed

A female client who has borderline personality disorder returns after a weekend pass with lacerations to both wrists. The client whines and complains to the nurse during the dressing change. How should the nurse respond?

A. Distant
B. Concerned
C. Matter-of-fact
D. Empathetic

1. Is the item written in a positive or a negative style?

2. Find the key words in the question.

3. Rephrase the question in your own words.

4. Rule out options:
   - ■
   - ■
   - ■

A client with bulimia is admitted to the mental health unit. What intervention is most important for the nurse to include in the initial treatment plan?

A. Observe client after meals for vomiting
B. Assess daily weight and vital signs
C. Monitor serum potassium and calcium
D. Provide a structured environment at mealtime

1. Is the item written in a positive or a negative style?

2. Find the key words in the question.

3. Rephrase the question in your own words.

4. Rule out options:
   - ■
   - ■
   - ■

EATING DISORDERS

Anorexia

- Voluntary refusal to eat and maintain minimal weight
- Distorted body image
- Fear of obesity with excessive dieting and exercise
- More common in females than males
- Occurs in adolescents and young adults
- Possible causes
  - Dysfunctional family system
  - Unrealistic expectations of perfection
  - Ambivalence about maturation and independence

Nursing Diagnoses
- Alteration in Nutrition
- Disturbance in Self-Concept
- Alteration in Family Process

Nursing Assessment
- Weight loss of at least 15% of ideal/original body weight
- Distorted body image
- Views self as fat
- Hair loss and dry skin
- Irregular heart rate
- ↓ Pulse and ↓ BP from ↓ fluid volume
- Amenorrhea for at least 3 months
- Delayed psychosexual development (adolescents)
- Disinterest in sex (adults)
- Dehydration and electrolyte imbalance resulting from
  — Diet pill abuse
  — Enema and laxative abuse
  — Diuretic abuse
  — Self-induced vomiting

Nursing Interventions
- Monitor weight, vital signs, and electrolytes
- Structure and support during mealtimes
- Set time limit for eating and monitor intake
- Monitor after meals for vomiting
- Be alert to client choosing low-calorie foods
- Monitor activity level to prevent excessive exercise
- Develop a behavior modification program

Bulimia Nervosa
- An eating disorder characterized by eating excessive amounts of food followed by self-induced vomiting
- Clients usually report a loss of control over eating during the bingeing
- Clients usually are not underweight

Assessment
- Diarrhea or constipation, abdominal pain, and bloating
- Dental damage (excessive vomiting)
- Sore throat; chronic inflammation of esophageal lining
- Concerns with body shape and weight

Nursing Interventions
- Monitor weight and electrolytes (esp. potassium)
- Provide structure around mealtime, observe after meals
- Encourage expression of feelings; family therapy
- Assist in learning to deal with feelings
- Discuss ways to stop vomiting/laxative use
- Positive reinforcement, build self-esteem
- Antidepressant medications as indicated

HESI Hint
Clients with anorexia gain pleasure from providing others with food and watching them eat. These behaviors reinforce their perception of self-control. Do not allow clients to plan or prepare food for unit activities.

- These disturbances in mood include depressive disorders, bipolar disorder, and manic depressive illness.
- Clients with depression have difficulty hearing and accepting compliments because they have lowered self-esteem.
- Depressive disorders occur on a continuum from mild to moderate to severe.

Depression
Symptoms

- Change in appetite with weight loss or gain
- Insomnia or hypersomnia
- Fatigue or a lack of energy
- Feelings of hopelessness, worthlessness
- Loss of ability to concentrate or think clearly
- Preoccupation with death or suicide
- Loss of interest or pleasure in life (cardinal symptom)

The nurse plans to assess the risk for suicide for a client who was admitted for depression. What question should the nurse ask first?
A. "Can you tell me how you are feeling now?"
B. "Have you ever tried to hurt yourself before?"
C. "Do you feel like hurting yourself now?"
D. "Do you have any plan for harming yourself?"

1. **Is the item written in a positive or a negative style?**

2. **Find the key words in the question.**

3. **Rephrase the question in your own words.**

4. **Rule out options:**
   -
   -
   -

Assessment
The MOST important assessment for depression: suicide risk

Obtain a History
- A previous attempt is the most important risk factor.
- Substance use, thought disorders, or other medical problems are other risk factors.

Be aware of major warning signs of impending attempt:
- Client begins to give away possessions
- Client becomes "better" or "happy"

NEVER leave a suicidal client alone!

Evaluating Suicidal Intent
- *Always* directly ask client if he or she is thinking of harming self
- If ideation is present, ask about plans and planned method
- Determine if the method is available

Note: The more lethal or readily available the method, the higher the probability of an attempt.

Antidepressant Medications

- Common tricyclic antidepressants
  - Amitriptyline (Elavil)
  - Clomipramine (Anafranil)
  - Desipramine (Norpramin)
  - Imipramine (Tofranil)
  - Nortriptyline (Aventyl)
  - Protriptyline (Vivactil)
  - Trimipramine (Surmontil)
- Common SSRIs
  - Citalopram (Celexa)
  - Escitalopram (Lexapro)
  - Fluvoxamine (Luvox)
  - Fluoxetine (Prozac)
  - Paroxetine (Paxil)
- Common monoamine oxidase inhibitors (MAOIs)
  - Phenelzine (Nardil)
  - Tranylcypromine (Parnate)
  - Selegiline transdermal patch (Emsam)

Purpose

Antidepressants have been approved for depression, phobias, and anxiety disorders.

Side Effects

- Anticholinergic effects (tricyclics)
  - Tachycardia
  - Dizziness
  - Insomnia
  - Drowsiness
  - Fluid retention
- Hypertensive crisis (MAOI)
  - Severe hypertension/headache
  - Chest pain and fever
  - Sweating, nausea, and vomiting
- SSRIs have fewer side effects than other antidepressants.
  - Drowsiness
  - Dizziness
  - Headache
  - Insomnia
  - Depressed appetite

Nursing Implications and Client Education

- Take 2 to 6 weeks for full therapeutic effectiveness
- Administer at bedtime to minimize sedative effects
- 2 to 5 weeks must lapse between stopping and starting new antidepressants
- MAOIs
  - Teach the client signs of hypertensive crisis
  - Must not be used with tricyclics
  - Need for dietary restrictions to avoid foods high in tyramine

Bipolar Disorder

Characterized by mood swings (e.g., life on a roller coaster) of euphoria, grandiosity, and an inflated sense of self-worth. The mood swings may or may not include depression.

Most clients with a mood disorder are not hospitalized. They generally receive outpatient treatment.

Symptoms of Mania

- Mild
  — Feeling of being "high"
  — Feeling of well-being
  — Usually does not seek treatment because of pleasurable effect
- Moderate
  — Grandiosity
  — Increased energy
  — Talkative
  — Pressured speech
  — Impulsiveness
  — Excessive spending
  — Bizarre dress or grooming
- Severe
  — Mania, flight of ideas
  — Continuous activity
  — Sexual acting out
  — Talkative
  — Easily distracted
  — Agitated, explosive
  — Delusions of grandeur

Communicating with a Manic Client

- Redirect negative behavior, set limits on intrusive behavior
- Be calm, firm, nonjudgmental, nondefensive
- Suggest a walk or physical activity
- "When you interrupt, I cannot talk to others; please wait your turn."
- Seclusion/medication can be used if a client is out of control
- Avoid arguing or becoming defensive

Mood-Stabilizing Medications

- Examples
  — Lithium carbonate (Lithotabs, Eskalith, Lithobid)
  — Divalproex sodium (Depakote)
  — Carbamazepine (Tegretol)
  — Gabapentin (Neurontin)
  — Topiramate (Topamax)
  — Lamotrigine (Lamictal)
  — Oxcarbazepine (Trileptal)

Review these medications in a nursing textbook or an NCLEX Review Manual:

- *Evolve Reach Comprehensive Review for the NCLEX-RN Examination* (powered by HESI)
- *Mosby's Comprehensive Review of Nursing for NCLEX-RN Examination*
- *Saunders Comprehensive Review for the NCLEX-RN Examination*

- Two atypical antipsychotic drugs (risperidone [Risperdal] and olanzapine [Zyprexa]) are also indicated for mania.
- Be familiar with common side effects and nursing implications for the various mood-stabilizing medications that may be used for these clients.

THOUGHT DISORDERS

Schizophrenia

A thought disorder characterized by altered thoughts and affect, withdrawal from reality, and difficulty with communication and relationships.

Nursing Assessment

- Hallucinations
  - False sensory perceptions
  - Most common are auditory and visual
  - Tactile occur with delirium
- Disorganized behavior
  - Disorganized, impulsive, and socially withdrawn
- Disorganized speech
  - Loose associations, tangential speech
  - Other speech patterns include echolalia, neologism, perseveration, or word salad
- Delusions
  - Fixed, false beliefs
  - Persecutory, grandiose, religious, or somatic

Nursing Diagnoses

- Disturbed Thought Processes
- Impaired Social Interactions
- Social Isolation
- Impaired Communication
- Disturbed Sensory-Perceptual

Nursing Interventions

- Delusions
  - Be matter-of-fact
  - Gently question the delusion—do not disagree/ agree
  - Focus on related feelings and reality-based topics
- Disorganized speech
  - DO NOT pretend to understand client's communication
  - Involve client in reality-based activities
  - Give simple directions for activities
- Hallucinations
  - Share observation of client hallucination
  - Observe nonverbal cues that hallucinations are present
  - If client hears voices, ask what they are saying
  - Assess for command hallucinations

Antipsychotic Medications

- Traditional medications
  - Purpose
    - Treat psychotic behavior
  - Side effects
    - Extrapyramidal
    - Anticholinergic
  - Nursing implications
    - Encourage fluid (water)
    - Gum
    - Hard candy
    - Increase fiber intake
- Long-acting medications
  - Purpose
    - Promote medication compliance
  - Side effects
    - Blood dyscrasias
    - Neuroleptic malignant syndrome
  - Nursing implications
    - Change position slowly for dizziness
    - Report urinary retention to healthcare provider
- Atypical medications
  - Purpose
    - Treat all positive and negative symptoms
  - Side Effects
    - Multiple side effects depending on medicatio
- Nursing Implications
  - Tolerance to effects usually occurs

Antipsychotic Medications

- First Generation
  - Phenothiazines
  - Chlorpromazine (Thorazine)
  - Fluphenazine (Prolixin)
  - Fluphenazine decanoate (Prolixin Decanoate)
  - Perphenazine (Trilafon)
  - Thioridazine (Mellaril)
  - Trifluoperazine (Stelazine)
  - Butyrophenone
  - Haloperidol (Haldol)
  - Haloperidol decanoate (Haldol Decanoate)
- Others
  - Loxapine (Loxitane)
  - Molindone (Moban)
  - Thiothixene (Navane)
- Seond Generation
  - Aripiprazole (Abilify)
  - Clozapine (Clozaril)
  - Olanzapine (Zyprexa)
  - Quetiapine (Seroquel)
  - Risperidone (Risperdal)
  - Ziprasidone (Geodon)

SUBSTANCE ABUSE

Alcoholism

- Assessments for withdrawal
  — Anxiety, nausea, tremors
  — Insomnia
  — Elevated pulse, BP, temp
  — Withdrawal can begin as eary as 4 to 6 hours after last drink
- Assessments for physical health
  — Chronic gastritis
  — Cirrhosis and hepatitis
  — Malnutrition
  — Dehydration
  — Pancreatitis

Nursing Interventions for Withdrawal

- Diazepam (Valium), clonazepam (Klonopin) for alcohol intoxication or withdrawal, and chlordiazepoxide (Librium) for alcohol withdrawal and anxiety
- Monitor vital signs q 4 hr or as ordered
- Reduce environmental stimuli
- Provide high-protein diet and adequate fluid intake (avoid caffeine)

Note: Priority intervention for chemically dependent clients is to monitor nutritional intake. Intake of alcohol and drugs impairs food intake.

Medication for Substance Use

- Disulfiram (Antabuse)
  — Deters client from drinking alcohol
  — Interferes with the breakdown of alcohol
  — Causes increased acetaldehyde and severe reactions
  — Clients must receive and sign informed consent about possible side effects when alcohol is ingested.
  — Any food, medications, or skin preparations with alcohol must be avoided.

A male client with a history of alcohol abuse is admitted to the medical unit for GI bleeding and pancreatitis. Admission data include: BP 156/96 mm Hg, pulse 92 bpm, and temperature 99.2° F. Which intervention is most important for the nurse to implement?
A. Provide a quiet, low-stimulus environment
B. Initiate seizure precautions
C. Administer PRN lorazepam (Ativan) as prescribed
D. Determine time and quantity of last alcohol intake

HESI Hint

The best therapy for chemically dependent clients is often provided by groups such as Alcoholics Anonymous, Narcotics Anonymous, etc.

HESI Hint

The client must be aware of hidden sources of alcohol!!

1. Is the item written in a positive or a negative style?

2. Find the key words in the question.

3. Rephrase the question in your own words.

4. Rule out options:
   -
   -
   -

Drug Use

- Pattern of use
  — What drugs
  — How much
  — How often
  — How long
- Physical evidence
  — Poor nutrition
  — Needle tracks
- Symptoms of withdrawal
  — Vary by substance

Note: Most common defense mechanisms (coping mechanisms) are denial, projection, and rationalization.

Nursing Diagnoses

- Risk for Injury
- Ineffective Coping
- Imbalanced Nutrition
- Deficient Fluid Volume
- Self-Care Deficit
- Social Isolation

Nursing Interventions

- Monitor vital signs
- Monitor I & O and electrolytes
- Provide adequate nutrition, hydration, and rest
- Administer medications per detoxification protocol
- Encourage expression of anger
- Identify stressors and areas of conflict
- Explore alternative coping

ABUSE

Child Abuse

- May include
  — Physical
  — Emotional
  — Sexual
  — Neglect
- Only one nurse should be assigned to an abused child because abused children have difficulty establishing trust.

Nursing Diagnoses

- Fear or Anxiety, Risk of Injury
- Powerlessness
- Interrupted Family Process, Alteration in Parenting

Nursing Assessment

- *Incongruent injury* with child's age/skills
- *Delay* in seeking medical care
- *Bruises:* unusual places, various stages of healing
- *Burns* (cigarette, iron): immersion burn (symmetrical shape)

HESI Hints
Withdrawal and Overdose

- Be aware of the types of illicit drugs and the symptoms of withdrawal and overdose.
- Do not forget that clients can withdraw and overdose using prescribed medications, such as the antianxiety drugs (and many others!).

HESI Hint

Developing trust and receiving care for their physical problems—these are the PRIMARY and IMMEDIATE needs of abused children.

- *Whiplash injuries* from being shaken
- *Bald patches,* hair has been pulled out
- *Fractures,* various stages of healing
- *Failure to thrive,* unattended physical problems

Nursing Interventions

- *Nurses are legally required to report all cases of suspected child abuse to the appropriate local/state agency.*
- Take color photographs of injuries
- Document factual, objective statements of child's physical condition, child-family interaction, and interviews
- Assess child-parent interaction

Intimate Partner Violence

- A criminal act of physical, emotional, economic, or sexual abuse
- Generally escalates in intensity and frequency
- Relationship usually characterized by extreme jealousy and issues of power and control
- Often begins during pregnancy and/or occurs more frequently during pregnancy

Nursing Assessment

- Delay between time of injury and time of treatment
- Anxious when answering questions about injury
- Depression and/or suicidal ideation
- Feels responsible for "provoking" spouse
- Abrasions, cuts, black eyes, sprains, and somatic complaints

Nursing Interventions

- Treat physical injuries
- Document factual, objective statements of client's physical condition and interactions with others
- Provide crisis intervention and refer to shelter if needed
- Assist client in contacting authorities if charges are pressed

Elder Abuse
Nursing Diagnosis

- Fear or Anxiety
- Risk of Injury
- Powerlessness
- Hopelessness
- Chronic Low Self-Esteem

Note: Often underreported and committed by spouses, children, and other caregivers

Nursing Assessment

- Bruises on upper arms (from being shaken)
- Dehydration, malnourishment, overmedication
- Poor physical hygiene, improper medical care
- Withdrawn, hopeless
- Demanding, belligerent, and aggressive behavior
- Repeated visits to physician for injuries/falls (e.g., broken bones)
- Injuries do not correlate with stated cause
- Misuse of money by children or legal guardians

Nursing Interventions

- Meet physical needs
- Document factual, objective statements of client's physical condition
- Report suspected abuse
- Arrange visiting nurses, nutrition services, or adult day care as needed
- THE NURSE MUST ESTABLISH TRUST WITH THE CLIENT!

Rape and Sexual Assault

- Sexual violence includes attempted or completed rape, sexual coercion and harassment, sexual contact with force or threat of force, and threat of rape.
- Often this violence occurs within the context of dating or acquaintance relationships, with the female partner the likely victim of violence and the male partner the likely perpetrator.

COGNITIVE DISORDERS

Cognitive disorders include delirium, dementia, and amnesic disorders.

Nursing Assessment

- Limited attention span, easily distracted
- Confusion, disorientation, impaired judgment
- Labile affect, may become suddenly angry
- Depression or anxiety
- Loss of recent and/or remote memory
- Increased psychomotor activity
- Decreased personal hygiene
- Sleep deprivation, day/night reversal

Nursing Interventions

- Maintain health, nutrition, safety, hygiene, and rest
- Encourage self-care
- Reinforce reality orientation
- Consistent environment
- Engage client in simple tasks to build self-esteem
- Refer to dementia, described in Chapter 9, Gerontological Nursing, for more interventions

HESI Hint

The most common defense is confabulation. The client uses confabulation to fill in memory gaps, decrease anxiety, and protect the ego.

Description of Delirium

■ Sudden onset
■ Short-term duration
■ Reversible
■ Poor memory and attention
■ Caused by specific stressor, such as infection, drugs, head trauma, electrolyte imbalance

Description of Dementia

■ Insidious and sporadic onset
■ Persistent duration
■ Irreversible, progressive
■ Lacks judgment, memory with altered thoughts
■ Caused by chronic alcoholism, vitamin B deficiency, HIV, Alzheimer's disease

Alzheimer's Medications

■ Acetylcholinesterase inhibitors
　— Tacrine (Cognex)
　— Donepezil (Aricept)
　— Rivastigmine (Exelon)
　— Galantamine (Reminyl)
　— Memantine (Namenda)
■ Atypical antipsychotics
　— Olanzapine (Zyprexa)
　— Quetiapine (Seroquel)
　— Risperidone (Risperdal)
■ Mood stabilizers and antianxiety agents as indicated

Childhood and Adolescent Disorders

■ Attention deficit (hyperactivity) disorder (ADD/ADHD)
■ Conduct disorder
■ Oppositional defiant disorder

An elderly male client is brought to the emergency department of an acute care hospital with recent memory loss, impaired coordination, sleep deprivation, and disorientation. Which health history finding suggests the client may be experiencing delirium?
A. Current and past treatment for alcohol abuse
B. Current treatment for Alzheimer's disease
C. Medication history with use of an antipsychotic
D. Treatment of Parkinson's disease for 5 years

Review these medications in a nursing textbook or an NCLEX Review Manual:
■ *Evolve Reach Comprehensive Review for the NCLEX-RN Examination* (powered by HESI)
■ *Mosby's Comprehensive Review of Nursing for NCLEX-RN Examination*
■ *Saunders Comprehensive Review for the NCLEX-RN Examination*

1. **Is the item written in a positive or a negative style?**

2. **Find the key words in the question.**

3. **Rephrase the question in your own words.**

4. **Rule out options:**
　■
　■
　■

9 Gerontological Nursing

The nurse is teaching an 86-year-old who has glaucoma and bilateral hearing loss. Which intervention should the nurse implement?
A. Maintain constant eye contact
B. Stand on the side unaffected by glaucoma
C. Speak in a lower tone of voice
D. Keep the environment dimly lit

PHYSIOLOGICAL CHANGES IN THE ELDERLY

- All cells are affected by aging
- Elderly clients
  - Will frequently complain that they do not sleep well
  - Have shorter sleep cycles
  - Awaken easily to environmental stimuli
  - Can experience further disorientation created by sleep medication

Cardiovascular Changes
- Systolic and diastolic BP increase but elevation of systolic is greater.
- Cardiac output decreases.
- Arteriosclerosis increases.
- Dysrhythmias can be more serious.
- Angina symptoms may be absent or confused as GI symptoms.

Teaching
- Avoid fatigue
- Low stress exercise
- Monitor BP
- Avoid extreme temperature changes
- Weigh daily
- Strict medication regimen

Respiratory Changes
- Lessened ability to cough and breathe deep
- Decreased pulmonary circulation
- Reduced respiratory efficiency
- Confusion (first sign of respiratory infection)
- COPD (chronic obstructive pulmonary disease), a major cause of respiratory disability
- Decreased humeral and cellular immunity; therefore increased risk of infection

1. Is the item written in a positive or a negative style?

2. Find the key words in the question.

3. Rephrase the question in your own words.

4. Rule out options:
  - ■
  - ■
  - ■

HESI Hints
- NCLEX-RN questions will focus on teaching clients about changes and rehabilitation programs.
- Remember to include exercise!

Teaching

- Pneumonia and flu vaccine
- STOP smoking
- Turning, deep breathing, and using incentive spirometer after procedures
- Pursed-lip breathing

Gastrointestinal Changes

- Lower esophageal sphincter relaxes leading to ↑ risk of aspiration
- ↓ Peristalsis, ↓ fluid intake, and ↓ mobility lead to constipation
- Simple sugars absorbed more slowly
- ↓ Absorption of vitamin B_1, vitamin B_2, and calcium

Teaching

- Assess teeth (tooth loss is NOT normal)
- Promote adequate bowel functioning
- Encourage regular exercise
- Encourage use of spices to ↑ taste sensation
- Watch for hidden sodium in food

Genitourinary Changes

- ↓ Renal function
- ↑ Risk for renal failure
- ↑ Urinary frequency related to decreased bladder capacity (tone and elasticity lost)
  — Capacity 500-600 mL down to 250 mL
- ↑ Frequency of infections
- ↓ Glucose reabsorption
- Prostatic enlargement

Teaching

- Use precaution with medications that are cleared by the renal system (PCN, digoxin, tetracycline)
- Kegel exercises
- Bladder training
- Skin care program for incontinence
- Fluid intake 2 to 3 L/day
- Antibiotic teaching for urinary tract infections (UTIs)

Reproductive Changes

- Perineal muscle weakness
- ↓ Estrogen production
- Menopause
- ↓ Testosterone production
- Sperm continue to be produced throughout lifetime
- Libido does not change in men or women

Teaching

- Perineal care
- Prescription creams for vaginal dryness
- Encourage annual digital examination for early identification of prostate cancer
- STD (sexually transmitted disease) prevention

Neurological Changes

- Neurological diseases are common:
  - — Alzheimer's disease
  - — Cardiovascular accident (CVA, stroke)
  - — Parkinson's disease
- ↓ Cerebral blood flow
- ↓ Ability to respond to multiple stimuli (reduced reflexes)
- Atrophy of taste buds
- Alteration in olfactory nerve
- Conductive hearing loss

Teaching

- Perform *complete* neurological assessment
- Find out what is "normal" for client
- Provide a SAFE environment
- Clots tend to form when client is just awakening; be alert for S/S of stroke
- Diet changes related to changes in sensory perception and dentition

Endocrine Changes

- ↓ Thyroid activity
- ↓ Aldosterone levels
- ↓ Metabolic rate
- ↓ T3 level
- Glucose intolerance
- Most common disorders: diabetes and thyroid dysfunction

Teaching

- Thyroid testing
- Memory cues to remember medications
- Diet and medication teaching if diabetes develops

Musculoskeletal Changes

- Bone loss
- Osteoporosis
- Fatigue more easily
- ↓ Lean body mass with ↑ body fat
- Cartilage erosion
- Decreased range of motion (ROM)

Teaching

- Adequate calcium intake
- Strengthening and weight-bearing exercise program
- Prevent falls
- Change positions slowly
- Adequate lighting
- Wear proper footwear

Integumentary Changes

- Thin skin
- Varicosities
- Poor circulation
- ↓ Ability for the skin to detect and regulate temperature
- Loss of elastin
- Brittle, thick nails

Teaching

- Lubricate skin
- Avoid powders
- Avoid excessive exposure to sunlight
- Good foot care
- Pad bony prominences

Sensory Changes

- ↓ Ability to accommodate for near vision
- ↓ Hearing ability
- ↓ Ability to distinguish tones
- ↓ Taste buds
- Cataracts
- Glaucoma

Teaching

- Encourage social interaction
- Use bright colors
- Large print
- Artificial tears
- Provide written material for teaching
- Face client when speaking
- Speak in lower tone
- Use spices for cooking

Integrity vs. Despair

Many losses occur:

- Spouse
- Job
- Friends
- Physical capacity
- Dementia

Teaching

- Determine current losses and those that have occurred in last 2 years
- Promote activities that build on past experiences
- Promote reminiscing
- Continuity of care

Dementia

- Most common are multi-infarct dementia and Alzheimer's disease
- Irreversible dementia has a gradual onset with a progressive downward course
- Be alert for false dementia brought about by:
  — Drug side effects
  — Depression
  — Poor nutrition
  — Metabolic disorders
- Interventions
  — Keep client actively involved as long as possible
  — Encourage orderly schedule to promote sense of security
  — Keep family pictures and familiar objects around to promote a sense of continuity
  — Speak slowly and calmly
  — Provide support for family and other caregivers

COMMON DISEASES OF THE ELDERLY

- Alzheimer's disease/dementia
- Cardiac dysrhythmias
- Arthritis
- Cataracts
- Glaucoma
- Brain attack (stroke)
- Graves' disease
- Delirium
- COPD
- UTI
- Depression

After stopping hormone replacement therapy (HRT), a 76-year-old reports she is experiencing increased vaginal discomfort during intercourse. What action should the nurse implement?
A. Suggest the use of a vaginal cream or lubricant
B. Recommend abstaining from sexual intercourse
C. Teach Kegel exercises daily
D. Instruct her to resume HRT

The spouse of a 94-year-old reports to the home health nurse that his wife has become increasingly confused over the last few days and has developed a cough. Which assessment should the nurse perform first?
A. Jugular vein distention
B. Skin turgor
C. Oxygen saturation
D. Pupillary response to light

HESI Hints

- Be aware of health maintenance guidelines for the elderly.
- Consider preventive teaching points for the elderly
- Be aware that the signs and symptoms of disease may be subtle, slower to develop, or very different from those seen in younger persons.

1. **Is the item written in a positive or a negative style?**

2. **Find the key words in the question.**

3. **Rephrase the question in your own words.**

4. **Rule out options:**
   -
   -
   -

1. **Is the item written in a positive or a negative style?**

2. **Find the key words in the question.**

3. **Rephrase the question in your own words.**

4. **Rule out options:**
   -
   -
   -

Appendix A
Normal Laboratory Values

TEST	ADULT	CHILD	INFANT/NEWBORN	ELDER	NURSING IMPLICATIONS
HEMATOLOGIC					
Hgb (hemoglobin): g/dL	Male: 14-18 Female: 12-16 Pregnant: <11	1-6 yr: 9.5-14 6-18 yr: 10-15.5	Newborn: 14-24 0-2 weeks: 12-20 2-6 months: 10-17 6 mo-1 yr: 9.5-14	Values slightly decreased	High-altitude living increases values. Drug therapy can alter values. Slight Hgb decreases normally occur during pregnancy.
Hct (hematocrit): %	Male: 42-52 Female: 37-47 Pregnant: >33	1-6 yr: 30-40 6-18 yr: 32-44	Newborn: 44-64 2-8 weeks: 39-59 2-6 months: 35-50 6 mo-1 yr: 29-43	Values slightly decreased	Prolonged stasis from vasoconstriction secondary to the tourniquet can alter values. Abnormalities in RBC size may alter Hct values.
RBC (red blood cell) count: million/mm^3	Male: 4.7-6.1 Female: 4.2-5.4	1-6 yr: 4-5.5 6-18 yr: 4.5-5	Newborn: 4.8-7.1 2-8 weeks: 4-6 2-6 months: 3.5-5.5 6 mo-1 yr: 3.5-5.2	Same as adult	Never draw specimen from an arm with an infusing IV. Exercise and high altitudes can cause an increase in values. Pregnancy values are usually lower. Drug therapy can alter values.
WBC (white blood cell) count: 1000/mm^3	Both sexes: 5-10	≤2 yr: 6.2-17 ≥2 yr: 5-10	Newborn, term: 9-30	Same as adult	Anesthetics, stress, exercise, and convulsions can cause increased values. Drug therapy can decrease values 24 to 48 hr postpartum; it is normal to have a count as high as 25.
Platelet count: 1000/mm^3	Both sexes: 150-400	150-400	Premature infant: 100-300 Newborn: 150-300 Infant: 200-475	Same as adult	Values may increase if living at high altitudes, exercising strenuously, or taking oral contraceptives. Values may decrease due to hemorrhage, DIC, reduced production of platelets, infections, prosthetic heart valves, and drugs (acetaminophen, aspirin, chemotherapy, H$_2$ blockers, INH, Levaquin, streptomycin, sulfonamides, thiazide diuretics).

(Continued)

TEST	ADULT	CHILD	INFANT/NEWBORN	ELDER	NURSING IMPLICATIONS
HESI Hint: Laboratory values that are most important to know for the NCLEX-PN exam are Hgb, Hct, WBCs, Na⁺, K⁺, BUN, blood glucose, ABGs (arterial blood gases), bilirubin for newborn, and therapeutic range for PT and PTT.					

TEST	ADULT	CHILD	INFANT/NEWBORN	ELDER	NURSING IMPLICATIONS
SED rate, ESR (erythrocyte sedimentation rate): mm/hr	Male: up to 15 Female: up to 20 Pregnant: ↑ all trimesters	Up to 10	Newborn: 0-2	Same as adult	Rate is elevated during pregnancy.
PT (prothrombin time): sec	Both sexes: 11-12.5 Pregnant: slight ↓	Same as adult	Same as adult	Same as adult	It is used in regulating Coumadin therapy. Therapeutic range is 1.5 to 2 times normal or control.
PTT (partial thromboplastin time): sec (see APTT)	Both sexes: 60-70 Pregnant: slight ↓	Same as adult	Same as adult	Same as adult	It is used in regulating heparin therapy. Therapeutic range is 1.5 to 2.5 times normal or control.
APTT (activated partial thromboplastin time): sec	Both sexes: 30-40	Same as adult	Same as adult	Same as adult	It is used in regulating heparin therapy. Therapeutic range is 1.5 to 2.5 times normal or control.

BLOOD CHEMISTRY					
Alkaline phosphatase: IU/L	Both sexes: 30-120	2-8 yr: 65-210 9-15 yr: 60-300 16-21 yr: 30-200	<2 yr: 85-235	Slightly higher than adult	Hemolysis of specimen can cause a false elevation in values.
Albumin: g/dL	Both sexes: 3.5-5 Pregnant: slight ↑	4.5-9	Premature infant: 3-4.2 Newborn: 3.5-5.4 Infant: 6-6.7	Same as adult	No special preparation is needed.
Bilirubin total: mg/dL	Total: 0.3-1 Indirect: 0.2-0.8 Direct: 0.1-0.3	Same as adult	Newborn: 1-12	Same as adult	Client is to be NPO except for water for 8 to 12 hr prior to testing. Prevent hemolysis of blood during venipuncture. Do *not* shake tube; it can cause inaccurate values. Protect blood sample from bright light.
Calcium: mg/dL	Both sexes: 9-10.5	8.8-10.8	<10 days: 7.6-10.4 Umbilical: 9-11.5 10 days-2 yr: 9-10.6	Values tend to decrease	No special preparation is needed. Use of thiazide diuretics can cause increased calcium values.
Chloride: mEq/L	Both sexes: 98-106	90-110	Newborn: 96-106 Premature infant: 95-110	Same as adult	Do not collect from an arm with an infusing IV solution.
Cholesterol: mg/dL	Both sexes: <200	120-200	Infant: 70-175 Newborn: 53-135	Same as adult	Do not collect from an arm with an infusing IV solution.

TEST	ADULT	CHILD	INFANT/NEWBORN	ELDER	NURSING IMPLICATIONS
CPK (creatine phosphokinase): IU/L	Male: 55-170 Female: 30-135	Same as adult	Newborn: 65-580	Same as adult	Specimen must not be stored prior to running test.
Creatinine: mg/dL	Male: 0.6-1.2 Female: 0.5-1.1	Child: 0.3-0.7 Adolescent: 0.5-1	Newborn: 0.2-0.4 Infant: 0.3-1.2	Decrease in muscle mass may cause decreased values	It is preferred but not necessary to be NPO 8 hr prior to testing. A ratio of 20:1 BUN to creatinine indicates adequate kidney functioning.
Glucose: mg/dL	Both sexes: 70-110	≤2 yr: 60-100 >2 yr: 7	Cord: 45-96 Premature infant: 20-60 Newborn: 30-60 Infant: 40-90	Increase in normal range after age 50	Client to be NPO except for water 8 hr prior to testing. Caffeine can cause increased values.
HCO$_3^-$: mEq/L	Both sexes: 23-30	20-28	Newborn: 13-22 Infant: 20-28	Same as adult	None
Iron: mcg/dL	Male: 80-180 Female: 60-160	50-120	Newborn: 100-250	Same as adult	It is preferred but not necessary to be NPO 8 hr prior to testing.
TIBC (total iron binding capacity): mcg/dL	Both sexes: 250-460	Same as adult	Same as adult	Same as adult	None
LDH (lactic dehydrogenase): IU/L	Both sexes: 100-190	60-170	Newborn: 160-450 Infant: 100-250	Same as adult	No IM injections are to be given 8 to 12 hr prior to testing. Hemolysis of blood will cause false positive result.
Potassium: mEq/L	Both sexes: 3.5-5	3.4-4.7	Newborn: 3-5.9 Infant: 4.1-5.3	Same as adult	Hemolysis of specimen can result in falsely elevated values. Exercise of the forearm with tourniquet in place may cause an increased potassium level.
Protein total: g/dL	Both sexes: 6.4-8.3	6.2-8	Premature infant: 4.2-7.6 Newborn: 4.6-7.4 Infant: 6-6.7	Same as adult	It is preferred but not necessary to be NPO 8 hr prior to testing.
AST/SGOT (aspartate aminotransferase): IU/L	0-35 Female slightly lower than adult males	3-6 yr: 15-50 6-12 yr: 10-50 12-18 yr: 10-40	0-5 days: 35-140 <3 yr: 15-60	Slightly higher than adult	Hemolysis of specimen can result in falsely elevated values. Exercise may cause an increased value.
ALT/SGPT (alanine aminotransferase): IU/mL	Both sexes: 4-36	Same as adult	Infant may be twice as high as adult	Slightly higher than adult	Hemolysis of specimen can result in falsely elevated values. Exercise may cause an increased value.

(*Continued*)

TEST	ADULT	CHILD	INFANT/NEWBORN	ELDER	NURSING IMPLICATIONS
Sodium: mEq/L	Both sexes: 136-145	136-145	Newborn: 134-144 Infant: 134-150	Same as adult	Do not collect from an arm with an infusing IV solution.
Triglycerides: mg/dL	Male: 40-160 Female: 35-135	6-11 yr: 31-108 12-15 yr: 36-138 16-19 yr: 40-163	0-5 yr: 30-86	Same as adult	Client is to be NPO 12 hr before testing. No alcohol for 24 hr before test.
BUN (blood urea nitrogen): mg/dL	Both sexes: 10-20	5-18	Newborn: 3-12 Cord: 21-40 Infant: 5-18	Slightly higher	None
ARTERIAL BLOOD CHEMISTRY					
pH	Both sexes: 7.35-7.45	Same as adult	Newborn: 3-12 Cord: 21-40 Infant: 5-18	Same as adult	Specimen must be heparinized. Specimen must be iced for transport. All air bubbles must be expelled from sample. Direct pressure to puncture site must be maintained.
Pco$_2$: mm Hg	Both sexes: 35-45	Same as adult	<2 yr: 26-41	Same as adult	Specimen must be heparinized. Specimen must be iced for transport. All air bubbles must be expelled from sample. Direct pressure to puncture site must be maintained.
Po$_2$: mm Hg	Both sexes: 80-100	Same as adult	Newborn: 60-70	Same as adult	Specimen must be heparinized. Specimen must be iced for transport. All air bubbles must be expelled from sample. Direct pressure to puncture site must be maintained.
HCO$_3^-$: mEq/L	Both sexes: 21-28	Same as adult	Infant/newborn: 16-24	Same as adult	Specimen must be heparinized. Specimen must be iced for transport. All air bubbles must be expelled from sample. Direct pressure to puncture site must be maintained.
O$_2$ Saturation: %	Both sexes: 95-100	Same as adult	Newborn: 40-90	95	Specimen must be heparinized. Specimen must be iced for transport. All air bubbles must be expelled from sample. Direct pressure to puncture site must be maintained.

From Pagana TJ, Pagana KD: *Mosby's Diagnostic and Laboratory Test Reference,* ed 8, St Louis, 2007, Mosby.

Practice Questions for the NCLEX-RN® Exam

Management/Leadership

1. **Which activity should the nurse delegate to an unlicensed assistive personnel (UAP)?**
   A. Check a client with cirrhosis to see if he can hear any better today after an IV antibiotic was discontinued.
   B. Push additional PO fluids for an elderly client with pneumonia who has developed a fever.
   C. Report the ability of a client with myasthenia gravis to manage the supper tray independently.
   D. Measure the liquid stool of a client who has received lactulose for an elevated serum NH3 level.

1. Is the item written in a positive or a negative style?

2. Find the key words in the question.

3. Rephrase the question in your own words.

4. Rule out options:
   ▪
   ▪
   ▪

2. **The nurse is delegating several client problems to the UAP. Which client requires the nurse to intervene? The client with**
   A. Active TB who is leaving the room without a mask.
   B. Dehydration who is requesting something to drink.
   C. Asthma who complains of being anxious and cannot concentrate.
   D. COPD who is leaving the unit to smoke as the next IVPB is due.

1. Is the item written in a positive or a negative style?

2. Find the key words in the question.

3. Rephrase the question in your own words.

4. Rule out options:
   ▪
   ▪
   ▪

3. **The nurse reports that a female client plans to unscrew the lightbulb in her room and try to cut herself. How should the charge nurse plan for nursing care?**
   A. Call in an extra nurse or technician for the next shift.
   B. Assign one of the current staff to be with the client.
   C. Move the client to another room with a roommate.
   D. The charge nurse should plan to care for this client.

1. Is the item written in a positive or a negative style?

2. Find the key words in the question.

3. Rephrase the question in your own words.

4. Rule out options:
   ▪
   ▪
   ▪

4. The unlicensed assistive personnel (UAP) is assisting with the care of eight clients on a postpartum unit. Which assignment should the nurse delegate to the UAP?
   A. Check fundal firmness and lochia for the clients who delivered vaginally.
   B. Take vital signs q 15 min for a client with pre-eclampsia.
   C. Provide breastfeeding instructions for a primigravida.
   D. Assist with daily care activities for clients on bed rest.

1. Is the item written in a positive or a negative style?

2. Find the key words in the question.

3. Rephrase the question in your own words.

4. Rule out options:
   ▪
   ▪
   ▪

Advanced Clinical Concepts

5. Which client is at the highest risk for respiratory complications?
   A. An 18-year-old with dehydration and cerebral palsy who is dependent in daily activities.
   B. A 60-year-old client with IDDM for 20 years who is admitted with cellulitis of the left leg.
   C. An obese 30-year-old with hypertension who is noncompliant with the medication regimen.
   D. A 40-year-old with a serum K^+ of 3.4 mEq/L who complains of fatigue while taking a loop diuretic.

1. Is the item written in a positive or a negative style?

2. Find the key words in the question.

3. Rephrase the question in your own words.

4. Rule out options:
   ▪
   ▪
   ▪

6. A nurse stops at an accident and finds a young adult male in an overturned truck that is leaking gasoline onto the hot pavement. The victim is pulseless and apneic. What action has the highest priority?
   A. Initiate basic life support.
   B. Remove the victim from the truck.
   C. Assess for hemorrhage.
   D. Remove glass shards from the face.

1. Is the item written in a positive or a negative style?

2. Find the key words in the question.

3. Rephrase the question in your own words.

4. Rule out options:
   ▪
   ▪
   ▪

7. The nurse observes that the IV infusion is empty for a client who has been vomiting during the immediate postoperative period. What action should the nurse implement?
   A. Hang a liter of D_5 ½ NS at the current rate.
   B. Use normal saline (NS) or lock the IV access.
   C. Maintain the infusion using a liter of ½ NS.
   D. Start a liter of D_5 LR at a keep-open rate.

1. Is the item written in a positive or a negative style?

2. Find the key words in the question.

3. Rephrase the question in your own words.

4. Rule out options:
   ▪
   ▪
   ▪

8. The nurse is administering a prescription for clotting factors for a client in shock. For which problem should the nurse plan the focus of care?
   A. Cardiac output
   B. Fluid volume deficit
   C. Infection
   D. Peripheral perfusion

1. Is the item written in a positive or a negative style?

2. Find the key words in the question.

3. Rephrase the question in your own words.

4. Rule out options:
   ■
   ■
   ■

9. A client's arterial blood gas results are pH 7.29, Pco_2 55 mm Hg, and HCO_3^- 26 mEq/L. Which compensatory response should the nurse expect this client to exhibit?
   A. Tachypnea
   B. Tachycardia
   C. Increased blood pressure
   D. Cerebral vasodilation

1. Is the item written in a positive or a negative style?

2. Find the key words in the question.

3. Rephrase the question in your own words.

4. Rule out options:
   ■
   ■
   ■

10. A client who has chronic back pain is not receiving adequate pain relief from oral analgesics. What alternative action should the nurse explore to promote the client's comfort and independence?
   A. Ask the healthcare provider to increase the analgesic dosage.
   B. Secure a prescription for a second analgesic by IV route.
   C. Consider the client's receptivity to use a TENS unit.
   D. Encourage counseling to avoid future addiction.

1. Is the item written in a positive or a negative style?

2. Find the key words in the question.

3. Rephrase the question in your own words.

4. Rule out options:
   ■
   ■
   ■

Maternal/Newborn Nursing

11. A 40-week gestational client is in active labor and calls the nurse to report her membranes ruptured. The nurse performs a sterile vaginal exam and discovers a prolapsed umbilical cord. Which intervention should the nurse implement first?
   A. Elevate the presenting fetal part off the cord.
   B. Cover the cord with sterile warm NS gauze.
   C. Prepare for an emergency cesarean birth.
   D. Start O_2 by facemask at 10 L/min.

1. Is the item written in a positive or a negative style?

2. Find the key words in the question.

3. Rephrase the question in your own words.

4. Rule out options:
   ■
   ■
   ■

12. A 39-week gestational client plans to have an epidural block when labor is established. What intervention should the nurse implement to prevent side effects?
    A. Teach about the procedure and effects of the epidural.
    B. Maintain the epidural infusion continuously throughout the second stage of labor.
    C. Administer a bolus of 500 to 1000 mL of a non-dextrose saline solution.
    D. Take vital signs every 30 minutes after the epidural medication is injected.

1. Is the item written in a positive or a negative style?

2. Find the key words in the question.

3. Rephrase the question in your own words.

4. Rule out options:
    ■
    ■
    ■

13. A female client presents in the emergency department complaining of RLQ abdominal pain and pain in her right shoulder. She has no vaginal bleeding, and her last menses was 6 weeks ago. Which action should the nurse implement first?
    A. Assess for abdominal rebound pain, distention, and fever.
    B. Obtain VS, IV access, and notify the healthcare provider.
    C. Observe for recent musculoskeletal injury, bruising, or abuse.
    D. Collect specimens for pregnancy test, hemoglobin, and WBC count.

1. Is the item written in a positive or a negative style?

2. Find the key words in the question.

3. Rephrase the question in your own words.

4. Rule out options:
    ■
    ■
    ■

14. A pregnant client with class III cardiac disease has hemoglobin of 10 g and a hematocrit of 28.7%. The nurse instructs the client to double her iron supplement, and she complains the extra iron will make her constipated. What explanation should the nurse offer?
    A. Constipation is caused by rising pregnancy hormones and crowding of the growing fetus, not the iron.
    B. Labor increases the workload of the heart, so stop the supplements 1 week before your due date.
    C. Anemia stresses the heart to work harder, so an abundant iron intake is needed to synthesize red blood cells.
    D. Bleeding during labor and delivery is expected and additional iron will be needed for erythropoiesis.

1. Is the item written in a positive or a negative style?

2. Find the key words in the question.

3. Rephrase the question in your own words.

4. Rule out options:
    ■
    ■
    ■

Medical/Surgical Renal

15. A client is returning to the unit after an intravenous pyelogram (IVP). Which intervention should the nurse include in the plan of care?
    A. Maintain bed rest
    B. Increase fluid intake
    C. Monitor for hematuria
    D. Continue NPO status

1. Is the item written in a positive or a negative style?

2. Find the key words in the question.

3. Rephrase the question in your own words.

4. Rule out options:
    ■
    ■
    ■

16. The nurse is teaching a client who has chronic urinary tract infections about a prescription for ciprofloxacin (Cipro) 500 mg PO bid. What side effect should the client not expect during the duration of medication therapy?
    A. Photosensitivity
    B. Dyspepsia
    C. Diarrhea
    D. Urinary frequency

1. Is the item written in a positive or a negative style?

2. Find the key words in the question.

3. Rephrase the question in your own words.

4. Rule out options:
    ■
    ■
    ■

17. Which client's complaints of pain require the nurse's intervention first? A client who is complaining of
    A. Bladder pain while receiving a continuous saline irrigant 2 hours after a transurethral prostatic resection.
    B. Incisional pain on the third day post-nephrectomy and requesting a PRN oral pain med.
    C. Flank pain that is partially relieved after passing a renal calculus.
    D. Bladder spasms after draining 1000 mL of urine during insertion of an indwelling catheter.

1. Is the item written in a positive or a negative style?

2. Find the key words in the question.

3. Rephrase the question in your own words.

4. Rule out options:
    ■
    ■
    ■

18. A male client with a Tenckhoff catheter calls to report he feels "poorly" and has a fever. What is the best response by the clinic nurse?
    A. Encourage him to come to the clinic today for assessment.
    B. Instruct him to increase his fluid intake to 3 L/day.
    C. Review his medication regimen for compliance.
    D. Inquire about his recent dietary intake of protein and iron.

1. Is the item written in a positive or a negative style?

2. Find the key words in the question.

3. Rephrase the question in your own words.

4. Rule out options:
    ■
    ■
    ■

Medical/Surgical Cardiovascular

19. The nurse is reviewing the cardiac markers for a client who is admitted after reporting chest pain that occurred last week. Which laboratory value elevation should the nurse identify as a late marker after myocardial injury?
    A. Troponin level
    B. Myoglobin level
    C. CK-MB levels
    D. LDH levels

1. Is the item written in a positive or a negative style?

2. Find the key words in the question.

3. Rephrase the question in your own words.

4. Rule out options:
    ■
    ■
    ■

20. The nurse is providing discharge instructions to a client who is diagnosed with angina pectoris. Which instruction is most important?
   A. Avoid activity that will involve the Valsalva maneuver.
   B. Seek emergency treatment if chest pain persists after the third nitroglycerin dose.
   C. Rest for 30 minutes after having chest pain before resuming activity.
   D. Keep extra nitroglycerin in an airtight and light-resistant bottle.

1. Is the item written in a positive or a negative style?

2. Find the key words in the question.

3. Rephrase the question in your own words.

4. Rule out options:
   ■
   ■
   ■

21. The nurse is providing discharge teaching for a client who is prescribed diltiazem (Cardizem). Which dietary instruction has the highest priority?
   A. Maintain a low-sodium diet
   B. Eat a banana each morning
   C. Ingest high-fiber foods daily
   D. Avoid grapefruit products

1. Is the item written in a positive or a negative style?

2. Find the key words in the question.

3. Rephrase the question in your own words.

4. Rule out options:
   ■
   ■
   ■

22. The nurse is teaching a young adult female who has a history of Raynaud's disease how to control her pain. What information should the nurse offer?
   A. Take oral analgesic at regularly spaced intervals.
   B. Avoid extremes of heat and cold.
   C. Limit foods and fluids with caffeine.
   D. Keep involved extremities in a dependent position.

1. Is the item written in a positive or a negative style?

2. Find the key words in the question.

3. Rephrase the question in your own words.

4. Rule out options:
   ■
   ■
   ■

23. The nurse is planning care for a client who is admitted with thrombocytopenia. Which nursing diagnosis best addresses this client's problem?
   A. Infection, risk for
   B. Injury, risk for bleeding
   C. Impaired nutrition, less than requirements
   D. Fatigue

1. Is the item written in a positive or a negative style?

2. Find the key words in the question.

3. Rephrase the question in your own words.

4. Rule out options:
   ■
   ■
   ■

Medical/Surgical Respiratory

24. A client who is admitted with cancer of the larynx is scheduled for a laryngectomy tomorrow. What is the top priority learning need for the client tonight?
    A. Body image counseling
    B. Pain management expectations
    C. Communication techniques
    D. Postoperative nutritional needs

1. Is the item written in a positive or a negative style?

2. Find the key words in the question.

3. Rephrase the question in your own words.

4. Rule out options:
   ▪
   ▪
   ▪

Psychiatric Nursing

25. A victim of a motor vehicle collision arrives in the Emergency Department dead on arrival. What action should the nurse implement to assist the spouse with this crisis?
    A. Ask if there are family, friends, or clergy to call.
    B. Talk about the former relationship with the spouse.
    C. Provide education about the stages of grief and loss.
    D. Assess the spouse's level of anxiety.

1. Is the item written in a positive or a negative style?

2. Find the key words in the question.

3. Rephrase the question in your own words.

4. Rule out options:
   ▪
   ▪
   ▪

26. The nurse is planning to lead a seminar for clinic and community health nurses on violence against women during pregnancy. Which statement describes an appropriate technique to assess for violence?
    A. Women should be assessed only if they are part of a high-risk group.
    B. Women may be assessed in the presence of young children, but not intimate partners.
    C. Women should be assessed once during pregnancy.
    D. Women should be reassessed face to face by a nurse as the pregnancy progresses.

1. Is the item written in a positive or a negative style?

2. Find the key words in the question.

3. Rephrase the question in your own words.

4. Rule out options:
   ▪
   ▪
   ▪

27. The charge nurse reminds several clients on the mental health unit that breakfast is at 8 AM, medications are given at 9 AM, and group therapy sessions begin at 10 AM. Which treatment modality has been implemented?
    A. Milieu therapy
    B. Behavior modification
    C. Peer therapy
    D. Problem solving

1. Is the item written in a positive or a negative style?

2. Find the key words in the question.

3. Rephrase the question in your own words.

4. Rule out options:
   ▪
   ▪
   ▪

28. The nurse is accompanying a male client to x-ray when he becomes panic stricken at the elevator and states, "I can't get on that elevator." Which action should the nurse implement first?
   A. Ask one more staff member to ride in the elevator.
   B. Offer an antianxiety medication.
   C. Begin desensitization about riding the elevator.
   D. Affirm his fears about riding the elevator.

1. Is the item written in a positive or a negative style?

2. Find the key words in the question.

3. Rephrase the question in your own words.

4. Rule out options:
   ■
   ■
   ■

29. A male client who experiences frequent nightmares and somnambulism is found one night trying to strangle his roommate. Which action that the nurse should implement has the highest priority?
   A. Give the client a sedative.
   B. Administer an antipsychotic.
   C. Move the client to a different room.
   D. Process with both clients about the event.

1. Is the item written in a positive or a negative style?

2. Find the key words in the question.

3. Rephrase the question in your own words.

4. Rule out options:
   ■
   ■
   ■

30. The nurse is updating the plan of care for a client who has a borderline personality disorder. Which intervention should be included with the nursing diagnosis of ineffective coping related to manipulation?
   A. Refer the client's requests to one nurse.
   B. Avoid challenging inappropriate behavior.
   C. Limit client's contact with other clients.
   D. Remove consequences for acting-out behaviors.

1. Is the item written in a positive or a negative style?

2. Find the key words in the question.

3. Rephrase the question in your own words.

4. Rule out options:
   ■
   ■
   ■

31. A female adolescent is admitted to the mental health unit for anorexia nervosa. What is the nurse's priority intervention?
   1. Teach about the importance of self-expression.
   2. Supervise activities during the day.
   3. Include in daily group therapy.
   4. Facilitate social interactions with others.

1. Is the item written in a positive or a negative style?

2. Find the key words in the question.

3. Rephrase the question in your own words.

4. Rule out options:
   ■
   ■
   ■

Practice Questions for the NCLEX-RN® Exam

32. The charge nurse is planning the daily schedule for clients on the mental health unit. To which activity group should a male client who is manic be assigned?
   1. Basketball game in the gym.
   2. Jogging at least 1 mile.
   3. Ping-pong game with peer.
   4. Group therapy with the art therapist.

1. Is the item written in a positive or a negative style?

2. Find the key words in the question.

3. Rephrase the question in your own words.

4. Rule out options:
   ■
   ■
   ■

ANSWERS AND RATIONALES

Management/Leadership

1. **Which activity should the nurse delegate to an unlicensed assistive personnel (UAP)?**

Rationales:

A. *Check a client with cirrhosis to see if he can hear any better today after an IV antibiotic was discontinued.*
   This requires assessment about ototoxicity which is beyond the scope of the UAP.

B. *Push additional PO fluids for an elderly client with pneumonia who has developed a fever.*
   These directions are not sufficiently clear and detailed for the UAP to perform the task.

C. *Report the ability of a client with myasthenia gravis to manage the supper tray independently.*
   This requires assessment of the client's clinical status that is beyond the scope of the UAP.

D. *Measure the liquid stool of a client who has received lactulose for an increased serum NH3 level.*
   This task encompasses basic care, elimination, and intake and output; it does not require judgment or the expertise of the nurse and can be performed by the UAP.

2. **The nurse is delegating several client problems to the UAP. Which client requires the nurse to intervene? The client with**

Rationales:

A. *Active TB who is leaving the room without a mask.*
   A UAP can be delegated to provide a box of masks, or to direct the client back to the room.

B. *Dehydration who is requesting something to drink.*
   A UAP can be directed to provide specific types and amounts of fluids.

C. *Asthma who complains of being anxious and cannot concentrate.*
   This client requires assessment and is at risk for airway compromise, which also requires assessment, so the nurse should respond to this client first.

D. *COPD who is leaving the unit to smoke as the next IVPB is due.*
   A UAP can ask the client to delay leaving the unit.

3. The nurse reports that a female client plans to unscrew the lightbulb in her room and try to cut herself. How should the charge nurse plan for nursing care?

Rationales:

A. *Call in an extra nurse or technician for the next shift.*

The charge nurse should plan ahead for staffing, but the immediate focus should be the client's safety now.

B. *Assign one of the current staff to be with the client.*

Since the client is at risk for suicide, the charge nurse should assign a staff member to stay with the client.

C. *Move the client to another room with a roommate.*

This will not ensure the client's safety, and a staff member must be present with the client at all times, not another client.

D. *The charge nurse should plan to care for this client.*

The charge nurse should not assume responsibility for the care of an individual client, since additional management responsibilities may interfere with the ability to ensure safe care.

4. The unlicensed assistive personnel (UAP) is assisting with the care of eight clients on a postpartum unit. Which assignment should the nurse delegate to the UAP?

Rationales:

A. *Check fundal firmness and lochia for the clients who delivered vaginally.*

Assessment is a responsibility of the nurse.

B. *Take vital signs q 15 min for a client with preeclampsia.*

This is a high-risk patient who needs to be evaluated by a licensed nurse.

C. *Provide breastfeeding instructions for a primigravida.*

Teaching is also the responsibility of the RN.

D. *Assist with daily care activities for clients on bed rest.*

This is the most appropriate assignment for the UAP. The RN should delegate daily care activities to the UAP based on the RN's assessments of each client's needs.

Advanced Clinical Concepts

5. Which client is at the highest risk for respiratory complications?

Rationales:

A. *An 18-year-old with dehydration and cerebral palsy who is dependent in daily activites.*

A client with dehydration and cerebral palsy (characterized by uncoordinated and spastic muscle movements) that causes significant involvement to affect ADL independence is at an increased risk for respiratory problems due to impaired mobility and impaired swallowing.

B. *A 60-year-old with IDDM for 20 years who is admitted with cellulitis of the left leg.*

This older client is more at risk for renal, cardiac, and vascular complications.

C. *An obese 30-year-old with hypertension who is noncompliant with the medication regimen.*

An obese adult who is noncompliant with antihypertensive medications is more at risk for cardiac or cerebral events than for respiratory problems.

D. *A 40-year-old with a serum K^+ of 3.4 mEq/L who complains of fatigue while taking a loop diuretic.*

This middle-aged adult is hypokalemic and fatigued, but is not at high risk for respiratory problems.

6. **A nurse stops at an accident and finds a young adult male in an overturned truck that is leaking gasoline onto the hot pavement. The victim is pulseless and apneic. What action has the highest priority?**

Rationales:

A. *Initiate basic life support.*

Although initiating CPR is vital to this victim's survival, it is not the first priority when there is the risk of explosion and fire.

B. *Remove the victim from the truck.*

The top priority is to remove the victim from the unsafe situation.

C. *Assess for hemorrhage.*

Accident victims are at risk for internal or external hemorrhage; however, this assessment does not have the highest priority.

D. *Remove glass shards from the face.*

Other life-threatening situations require action before the removal of glass.

7. **The nurse observes that the IV infusion is empty for a client who has been vomiting during the immediate postoperative period. What action should the nurse implement?**

Rationales:

A. *Hang a liter of D_5 ½ NS at the current rate.*

This action is not recommended because hypertonic solutions are prescribed for fluid and electrolyte imbalances and cause an osmotic movement of fluids into the vasculature.

B. *Use normal saline (NS) or lock the IV access.*

The nurse should maintain the IV access with an isotonic solution, such as NS, for intravascular fluid volume replacement or lock the access until further prescriptions are available.

C. *Maintain the infusion with a liter of ½NS.*

This is not a recommended action because this hypotonic solution is prescribed for cellular dehydration, not postoperative fluid volume deficit.

D. *Start a liter of D_5 LR at a keep-open rate.*

This is not a recommended action because a hypertonic solution will cause an osmotic movement of fluids into the vascular space and contribute to fluid and electrolyte imbalances.

8. **The nurse is administering a prescription for clotting factors for a client in shock. For which problem should the nurse plan the focus of care?**

Rationales:

A. *Cardiac output*

Cardiogenic shock is the result of the heart failing as a pump.

B. *Fluid volume deficit*

Hypovolemic shock is the result of fluid volume loss, either from the body or due to third spacing.

C. *Infection*

The nurse should focus the plan of care on infection. Septic shock results from toxins circulating in the vascular bed that cause the clotting factors to pool in the microcirculation, leaving the client vulnerable to bleeding due to insufficient factors in the larger vessels, i.e., disseminating intravascular coagulation (DIC).

D. *Peripheral perfusion*

Vasogenic shock is similar to hypovolemic shock because generalized vasodilation results in insufficient blood volume in the "now" enlarged vascular tree, which results in a reduced hydrostatic pressure with inadequate baroreceptor response.

9. **A client's arterial blood gas results are pH 7.29, Pco_2 55 mm Hg, and HCO_3^- 26 mEq/L. Which compensatory response should the nurse expect this client to exhibit?**

Rationales:

A. *Tachypnea*

The client is experiencing respiratory acidosis and will demonstrate hyperventilation as a compensatory mechanism to remove excess CO_2.

B. *Tachycardia*

Acid-base imbalances are compensated primarily by the lungs and the renal system. Plasma proteins and ionic shifts (intracellular) also serve as buffering systems. Tachycardia (B), increased BP (C), and cerebral vasodilation (D) do not serve as compensatory mechanisms.

C. *Increased blood pressure*

See rationale for option B.

D. *Cerebral vasodilation*

See rationale for option B.

10. **A client who has chronic back pain is not receiving adequate pain relief from oral analgesics. What alternative action should the nurse explore to promote the client's comfort and independence?**

Rationales:

A. *Ask the healthcare provider to increase the analgesic dosage.*

While this intervention may improve pain relief, it may not promote self-care without increasing side effects that may affect the client's independence.

B. **Secure a prescription for a second analgesic by IV route.**
The IV route does not promote self-care and also may cause additional side effects that interfere with the client's ability to carry out ADLs independently.

C. **Consider the client's receptivity to use a TENS unit.**
This action supports increased pain control and self-care without the high level of adverse effects associated with additional medication. It is the least invasive measure, and promotes the active participation (self-care) of the client.

D. **Encourage counseling to avoid future addiction.**
Referrals may be needed, but the nurse should teach clients about potential problems with medications and measures to manage pain and maintain self-care.

Maternal/Newborn Nursing

11. **A 40-week gestational client is in active labor and calls the nurse to report her membranes ruptured. The nurse performs a sterile vaginal exam and discovers a prolapsed umbilical cord. Which intervention should the nurse implement first?**

Rationales:

A. **Elevate the presenting fetal part off the cord.**
This action is the most critical intervention; the nurse must prevent compression of the cord by the presenting part, which will impair fetal circulation, leading to both morbidity and death.

B. **Cover the cord with sterile warm NS gauze.**
If the cord is protruding outside the vagina, this should be implemented to prevent drying of the Wharton's jelly. However, another nurse should do this while the nurse maintains elevation of the presenting part off the cord.

C. **Prepare for an emergency cesarean birth.**
This is implement by the staff while the nurse maintains the presenting part off the cord.

D. **Start O$_2$ by facemask at 10 L/min.**
Oxygen should be provided to the mother to increase oxygen delivery to the fetus via the placenta, but another nurse should implement this while the nurse maintains the presenting part off the cord.

12. **A 39-week gestational client plans to have an epidural block when labor is established. What intervention should the nurse implement to prevent side effects?**

Rationales:

A. **Teach about the procedure and effects of the epidural.**
Teaching is an important nursing intervention to alleviate anxiety, but it does not prevent hypotension, a side effect due to vasodilatation caused by the epidural block.

B. **Maintain the epidural infusion continuously throughout the second stage of labor.**
Difficulty in internal rotation of the fetal head may occur because of relaxation of the pelvic floor, caused by the epidural, and therefore it may be necessary to discontinue the epidural infusion during transition or at the end of stage I.

C. **Administer a bolus of 500 to 1000 mL of a non-dextrose saline solution.**
Prehydration will increase maternal blood volume and prevent hypotension, which occurs due to vasodilatation, a side effect of epidural anesthesia. A non-dextrose solution is used to prevent fetal secretion of insulin that later places the neonate at risk for hypoglycemia.

D. **Take vital signs every 30 minutes after the epidural medication is injected.**
Vital signs should be monitored every 5 minutes immediately after the initial epidural dose, and if stable, then every 15 minutes.

13. **A female client presents in the Emergency Department complaining of RLQ abdominal pain and pain in her right shoulder. She has no vaginal bleeding, and her last menses was 6 weeks ago. Which action should the nurse implement first?**

Rationales:

A. **Assess for abdominal rebound pain, distention, and fever.**
Bleeding related to an ectopic pregnancy (based on the client's history) may present these manifestations, but the nurse should first assess the client for hypovolemic shock.

B. **Obtain VS, IV access, and notify the healthcare provider.**
The nurse should first evaluate the client for vital sign changes of shock due to a ruptured ectopic pregnancy (an obstetrical emergency). A vascular access is vital in an emergency situation, and the healthcare provider should be notified immediately.

C. **Observe for recent musculoskeletal injury, bruising, or abuse.**
This may be part of the assessment if a life-threatening situation is ruled out first.

D. **Collect specimens for pregnancy test, hemoglobin, and WBC count.**
A pregnancy test and CBC specimens should be collected, but the nurse should first notify the healthcare provider of the client's status based on the presenting vital signs and symptoms of bleeding, as manifested by intra-abdominal bleeding that collects under the diaphragm causing referred shoulder pain.

14. **A pregnant client with class III cardiac disease has hemoglobin of 10 g and a hematocrit of 28.7%. The nurse instructs the client to double her iron supplement, and she complains the extra iron will make her constipated. What explanation should the nurse offer?**

Rationales:

A. *Constipation is caused by rising pregnancy hormones and crowding of the growing fetus, not the iron.*

Oral iron supplements cause the stool to become tenacious and contribute to constipation.

B. *Labor increases the workload of the heart, so stop the supplements 1 week before your due date.*

This does not explain the need for the additional iron.

C. *Anemia stresses the heart to work harder, so extra iron is needed to synthesize red blood cells.*

The nurse should explain that the heart works harder to pump inadequate numbers of RBCs, so extra iron is needed to produce more cells to carry adequate oxygen to tissues and thereby reduce the workload of the heart.

D. *Bleeding during labor and delivery is expected and additional iron will be needed for erythropoiesis.*

Additional iron should be made available for erythropoiesis, after delivery; however, the client's cardiac disease is the underlying reason to treat anemia.

Medical/Surgical Renal

15. **A client is returning to the unit after an intravenous pyelogram (IVP). Which intervention should the nurse include in the plan of care?**

Rationales:

A. *Maintain bed rest*

There is no need to restrict mobility after an IVP.

B. *Increase fluid intake*

The client should increase the intake of fluids to adequately clear the dye used in an IVP because the dye may damage the kidneys.

C. *Monitor for hematuria*

There is no risk of hematuria related to the IVP.

D. *Continue NPO status*

The client does not need to be NPO after an IVP. Fluids should be increased.

16. **The nurse is teaching a client who has chronic urinary tract infections about a prescription for ciprofloxacin (Cipro) 500 mg PO bid. What side effect should the client not expect during the duration of medication therapy?**

Rationales:

A. *Photosensitivity*

This is not a side effect of Cipro; however, the nurse should instruct clients to avoid exposure to the sun when this is a risk or side effect of a medication.

B. *Dyspepsia*

Cipro causes GI irritation, nausea and vomiting, and abdominal pain, which should be reported.

C. *Diarrhea*

Watery, foul-smelling diarrhea is an adverse reaction of Cipro that is an indicator of pseudomembranous colitis, which should be reported and requires immediate intervention.

D. **Urinary frequency**
   Urinary frequency may indicate that the medication is ineffective and should be reported.

17. **Which client's complaints of pain require the nurse's intervention first? A client who is complaining of**

Rationales:

A. *Bladder pain while receiving a continuous saline irrigant 2 hours after a transurethral prostatic resection.*
   This client is at risk of clot formation occluding the catheter, which may indicate bleeding and bladder distention, and the nurse should evaluate this client immediately.

B. *Incisional pain on the third day post-nephrectomy and requesting a PRN oral pain med.*
   This is not as high a priority compared to option A because the client is not at risk of any altered homeostasis.

C. *Flank pain that is partially relieved after passing a renal calculus.*
   This client's condition is not likely to worsen now that the stone was passed, and should be evaluated after the client in option A.

D. *Bladder spasms after draining 1000 mL of urine during insertion of an indwelling catheter.*
   This client's pain reflects bladder spasms and is of lower priority than option A.

18. **A male client with a Tenckhoff catheter calls to report he feels "poorly" and has a fever. What is the best response by the clinic nurse?**

Rationales:

A. *Encourage him to come to the clinic today for assessment.*
   Tenckhoff catheters are used in peritoneal dialysis. They are often used at home by the client, placing the client at risk for peritoneal infection. Because dialysis clients usually have some degree of compromised immunity and anemia, he should be assessed and should come to the clinic.

B. *Instruct him to increase his fluid intake to 3 L/day.*
   Client who need dialysis retain fluid and usually are restricted to a 300-mL intake greater than output.

C. *Review his medication regimen for compliance.*
   The nurse should evaluate the client's compliance, but assessing the client for infection is a greater priority.

D. *Inquire about his recent dietary intake of protein and iron.*
   Iron deficiency and protein loss are common problems in clients who are receiving peritoneal dialysis. Dietary intake is important but does not hold a higher priority than possible infection.

19. The nurse is reviewing the cardiac markers for a client who is admitted after reporting chest pain that occurred last week. Which laboratory value elevation should the nurse identify as a late marker after myocardial injury?

Rationales:

A. *Troponin level*

   Troponin is released quickly from injured myocardial tissue but will fall after 3 to 4 days and slowly return to normal levels. Troponin levels are the most immediate and specific cardiac biomarker.

B. *Myoglobin level*

   Whole myoglobin starts to increase in about 3 hours after MI, but it is not as sensitive as other markers and can rise even after skeletal muscle injury, such as occurs with IM injection, and returns to normal in 2 days.

C. *CK-MB levels*

   This isoenzyme is useful in supporting MI, determining the extent and time of the infarct. This marker usually returns to normal in 72 hours and is less useful in the nonacute phase.

D. *LDH levels*

   After myocardial injury, this level rises in 24 to 48 hours, and returns to normal in about 5 to 10 days. Isolated elevation of this isoenzyme is especially useful as a delayed indicator of myocardial injury.

20. The nurse is providing discharge instructions to a client who is diagnosed with angina pectoris. Which instruction is most important?

Rationales:

A. *Avoid activity that will involve the Valsalva maneuver.*

   While minimizing or avoiding the Valsalva maneuver will decrease anginal pain, it is not the most important factor.

B. *Seek emergency treatment if chest pain persists after the third nitroglycerin dose.*

   This instruction has the most importance because chest pain characteristic of acute MI persists longer than 15 minutes, and delaying medical treatment can be life threatening.

C. *Rest for 30 minutes after having chest pain before resuming activity.*

   Waiting 30 minutes may be recommended only if the nitroglycerin is effective in relieving the chest pain.

D. *Keep extra nitroglycerin in an airtight and light-resistant bottle.*

   This is excellent medication teaching, but it does not have the same urgency as seeking emergency care.

21. The nurse is providing discharge teaching for a client who is prescribed diltiazem (Cardizem). Which dietary instruction has the highest priority?

Rationales:

A. *Maintain a low-sodium diet.*
The client may need to restrict sodium intake, but it is not specific for Cardizem.

B. *Eat a banana each morning.*
If the client has low potassium, this should be recommended.

C. *Ingest high-fiber foods daily.*
This is an excellent teaching point for everyone, but is not specific for Cardizem.

D. *Avoid grapefruit products.*
Grapefruit should be avoided when taking calcium channel blockers because it can cause an increase in the serum drug level, predisposing the client to hypotension.

22. **The nurse is teaching a young adult female who has a history of Raynaud's disease how to control her pain. What information should the nurse offer?**

Rationales:

A. *Take oral analgesic at regularly spaced intervals.*
Pain is not always associated with Raynaud's disease, but rather the feeling of cold hands and fingers and pallor. If pain is sporadic or situational, it should not necessitate regular use of analgesia.

B. *Avoid extremes of heat and cold.*
In Raynaud's disease, vascular spasms of the hands/fingers are triggered by exposure to extremes of heat or cold, which causes the characteristic pallor and cold-to-touch symptoms of the upper extremities.

C. *Limit foods and fluids with caffeine.*
Caffeine is not the primary trigger of the episodes, but if the client notes that caffeine contributes to the blanching and coldness, caffeine should be avoided.

D. *Keep involved extremities in dependent position.*
This is not effective for the client with Raynaud's disease.

23. **The nurse is planning care for a client who is admitted with thrombocytopenia. Which nursing diagnosis best addresses this client's problem?**

Rationales:

A. *Infection, risk for*
This is indicated for a client with neutropenia.

B. *Injury, risk for bleeding*
Thrombocytopenia refers to a low platelet count. Platelets are essential for initiating the normal clotting mechanism. This client is at risk for injury and bleeding.

C. *Impaired nutrition, less than requirements*
Nutrition should be addressed to ensure adequate iron intake, but this is not the present problem.

D. *Fatigue*
Fatigue is a problem associated with anemia.

Medical/Surgical Respiratory

24. A client who is admitted with cancer of the larynx is scheduled for a laryngectomy tomorrow. What is the top priority learning need for the client tonight?

Rationales:

A. Body image counseling

This is a concern after surgery when the immediate life-threatening insult of cancer is assimilated and basic needs are met.

B. Pain management expectations

Pain relief expectations are a priority, but the inability to convey (communicate) a subjective symptom, such as pain, is the fear the client perceives first.

C. Communication techniques

A client who is in crisis and anticipating the immediate postoperative period is concerned with immediate needs, such as the ability to express, convey, and obtain intervention.

D. Postoperative nutritional needs

Nutrition is important to promote healing, but the ability to communicate one's subjective needs is a higher priority.

Psychiatric Nursing

25. A victim of a motor vehicle collision arrives in the Emergency Department dead on arrival. What action should the nurse implement to assist the spouse with this crisis?

Rationales:

A. Ask if there are family, friends, or clergy to call.

The nurse should help the spouse identify support systems and resources that are helpful while coping with a crisis situation, such as the sudden death of a spouse.

B. Talk about the former relationship with the spouse.

The spouse may be unable to process information during the crisis, and the nurse should focus on immediate needs for coping and support.

C. Provide education about the stages of grief and loss.

Educating the client about grief and loss is not an immediate priority in the crisis and should be provided after the spouse begins to cope with the crisis.

D. Assess the spouse's levels of anxiety.

Although the nurse should assess the spouse for anxiety, the immediate approach should include a directive approach to assist the spouse in dealing with the stressful event.

26. The nurse is planning to lead a seminar for clinic and community health nurses on violence against women during pregnancy. Which statement describes an appropriate technique to assess for violence?

Rationales:

A. *Women should be assessed only if they are part of high-risk groups.*
   Violence against women occurs in all ethnic groups and at all income levels.

B. *Women may be assessed in the presence of young children, but not intimate partners.*
   It is important to assess women without their partners present; it is also important that verbal children not be present, as they may repeat what is heard. Infants may be present.

C. *Women should be assessed once during pregnancy.*
   Many women do not reveal violence the first time they are asked. As trust develops between nurse and client, the client may be more comfortable sharing her story. Also, violence may start later in the pregnancy.

D. *Women should be reassessed face to face by a nurse as the pregnancy progresses.*
   More than one face-to-face interview elicits the highest reports of violence during pregnancy.

27. **The charge nurse reminds several clients on the mental health unit that breakfast is at 8 AM, medications are given at 9 AM, and group therapy sessions begin at 10 AM. Which treatment modality has been implemented?**

Rationales:

A. *Milieu therapy*
   Milieu therapy uses resources and activities in the environment to assist with improving social functioning and activities of daily living.

B. *Behavior modification*
   Behavior modification involves changing behaviors with positive and negative reinforcements to allow desired activities or remove privileges.

C. *Peer therapy*
   Peer therapy is not a single therapeutic modality, but utilizes peers who are responsible for supporting, sharing, and compromising within their peer group and milieu.

D. *Problem solving*
   Problem solving is used in crisis intervention and focuses on the problem identification and ways to return to prior levels of functioning.

28. **The nurse is accompanying a male client to x-ray when he becomes panic stricken at the elevator and states, "I can't get on that elevator." Which action should the nurse implement first?**

Rationales:

A. *Ask one more staff member to ride the elevator.*
   One more staff member will not be able to mobilize the client to ride the elevator because he must first recognize his feelings about the phobia and accept the need to change his behavior.